THE BEST IN

TRADE & EXHIBITION
STAND DESIGN

THE BEST IN

TRADE & EXHIBITION
STAND DESIGN

CONSULTANT EDITOR
STAFFORD CLIFF

ROTOVISION

A QUARTO BOOK

Published by ROTOVISION SA
Route Suisse 9
CH-1295 Mies
Switzerland

Distributed to the trade in the
United States & Canada by
Watson-Guptill Publications
1515 Broadway
New York, NY 10036

ISBN 0–8230–6072–1

This book was designed and produced by
Quarto Publishing plc
6 Blundell Street
London N7 9BH

Creative Director: Richard Dewing
Designer: Chris Dymond
Editor: Viv Croot

Typeset in Great Britain by
Central Southern Typesetters, Eastbourne
Manufactured in Hong Kong by Regent Publishing Services Limited
Printed in Hong Kong by Leefung-Asco Printers Ltd

This book is dedicated to Sir Terence Conran, for
whom I have designed many exhibitions, and
Suzanne Slesin and Priscilla Carluccio, with whom
I've tramped many an exhausting Trade Fair.
I would also like to acknowledge the help of
Ann Berne, Virginia Christensen, Virginia Pepper,
John Ronayne, Jonathan Scott.

Contents

Introduction

Exhibition design is a very broad subject with a rich history to it. The Great Exhibition in London's Hyde Park in 1851, the Paris Exposition of 1925, the World's Fair, Disneyland and Disneyworld, travelling funfairs and local agricultural shows are all familiar examples of exhibition design, even though they vary hugely in scale and subject.

Currently there is an enormous increase in the number of exhibitions being staged. London's Victoria and Albert Museum and Hayward Gallery, New York's Metropolitan and Museum of Modern Art all have expensive and long-term programmes planned.

At the same time, dozens of local councils and institutions are looking for ways to attract more visitors; creating an exhibition about the history of the area is proving a popular solution. Old farmhouses and isolated villages, decommissioned factories and mills of all kinds, outworked mines and redundant breweries are turned into imaginative recreations of the past where local people are employed to demonstrate traditional crafts and revive long forgotten skills.

Trade and tourism also rely heavily on exhibition design. In Tokyo most department stores include a floor devoted to exhibitions, and in France the FNAC retail group hold

The Palace of Commerce
New York City, New York, USA

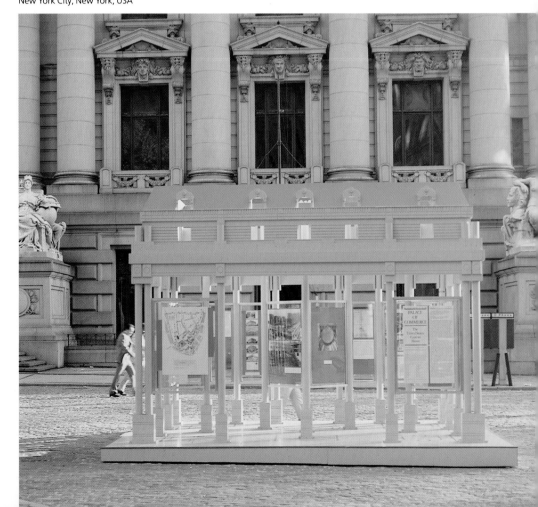

La Cité-Ciné
La Villette, Paris, France

changing exhibitions of photography in their shops. In 1992, the World's Fair in Seville, Spain will employ dozens of design companies and creative consultants working on 94 pavilions for over 100 countries. It was predicted that 40 million people would attend the Fair during its six-month run, an enormous number for a city whose population is less than one tenth of New York City, where the World's Fair of 1939 attracted 43 million visitors.

The other side of the coin is the commercial exhibition and Trade Fair. Every year (sometimes twice) manufacturers, suppliers, agents and all kinds of service industries spend more and more money striving to outdo their competitors and impress their customers with lavish, often very shortlived displays of their products and services.

Some exhibitions – 'Tutankhamun' at the British Museum in London or 'La Cité Ciné' at La Villette in Paris – remain in our memory for years afterwards; but often the design of an exhibition is overshadowed by the exhibits themselves and for this reason is often taken for granted. After all, it's the exhibits that people go to see, even if it is more often the dramatic lighting, simple explanatory graphics or clever presentation that helps to make the impact and tells the story in a way that anyone can easily understand.

BMW Stand
International Motor Show 1988, Birmingham, England

New ideas for special effects to make this impact even more powerful are being dreamt up every day by exhibition designers. For example, in 'The City and its Port' exhibition at London's Tower Hill, life in the 18th century shipbuilding industry is accentuated by the use of 13 different chemically created smells including sea breezes, furniture polish, freshly cut pine and sweaty sailors.

The Walt Disney Corporation has been one of the first in the field of continual developments of more and more sophisticated animatronics and special effects. They were among the first to develop the 'dark ride' technique where visitors are taken on an automated journey, much as they were in the old-fashioned ghost trains of seaside funfairs. And in Los Angeles, the Universal Studios tour includes an earthquake in a San Francisco subway station, during which an oncoming train jumps the rails, jacknifes and comes to rest only inches from the audience. Simultaneously, the roof of the station splits apart and the platform is deluged with 60,000 gallons of water. All this takes only 15-20 seconds to recycle and return to normal before the next visitors arrive.

Many exhibition design companies employ special effects designers whose job it is to create illusions. Fibre optics and video monitors are used to illustrate the cycle of water, images are projected onto a curtain of mist and — with the help of mirrors — cars are made to appear and disappear out of thin air.

In spite of all this ingenuity, the one piece of technology that could really transform the industry is Virtual Reality. With the help of computer-simulated 3D worlds, visitors will be able to experience and interact with images which exist only within their headpiece. For a car launch event, they could get into the (virtual) car and drive it over any terrain anywhere in the (virtual) world. Whole exhibitions could be created in Virtual Reality once the quality of the imagery and the equipment has been perfected.

So where does this leave the designer? Still sitting at the drawing board with a sharpened 3B, I suspect. The panic that followed the introduction of CAD was unjustified, and the perfection of Virtual Reality is unlikely to signal the redundancy of the designer; on the contrary, it will probably mean that craftspeople – ideas people – will be more important than ever. After all, the slickest presentation technique, or the most brilliant computer-generated imagery will never compensate for – or hide – the lack of a good idea or an original thought.

The Blitz Experience
The Imperial War Museum, London, England

Galleries and Museums

The best work is often by design teams and exhibition specialists working closely with — and sometimes permanently employed by — some of the world's largest galleries and museums. Some exhibitions are so popular that visitors are required to book tickets for a specific day and time weeks in advance, as were visitors to the 1990 Van Gogh Exhibition in Amsterdam. The Picasso Exhibition at New York's Museum of Modern Art was so difficult to get into that the T-shirts bought at the show quickly became status symbols.

International Red Cross and Red Crescent Museum

PROJECT: Exhibition of International Humanitarian History from 1850 to today through the activities of the International Red Cross and Red Crescent Movement.

DATE AND LOCATION: 1988, Geneva, Switzerland

PERMANENT, TRAVELLING OR ONE-OFF: Permanent, with additional temporary exhibitions every six months.

SIZE (METRES OR FEET): 3460 sq m on three levels: 2045 sq m for permanent exhibits; 215 sq m for temporary exhibitions

DESIGNER: Architects: Pierre Zoelly, Georges Haefeli, Michel Girardet; Graphics, Design and Staging: Atelier Roger Pfund/Sophie Jordi, Roland Aeschilimann, Antoine Cahen, Claude Froddard; Audiovisual Design: Henri Chenaux.

BRIEF: To share the remarkable experience of men and women who for over a century have been living their mission at the service of mankind.

ATTENDANCE: Public

Red Cross + Red Crescent Museum

Henry Dunant, a Genevese businessman, was so
appalled by the suffering of the wounded at the
battle of Solferino (1859) that he was inspired to
found the Red Cross in 1863. The statue, by George
Segal, shows Dunant drawing up the proposal
which was to form the basis of the Geneva
Convention.

14

pas à souhaiter qu'ils
de congrès pour formuler
conventionnel et
et ratifié, servirait
secours pour
? Il est

Imperial War Museum

PROJECT: The Trench Experience

DATE AND LOCATION: 1990, Imperial War Museum, London, England

PERMANENT, TRAVELLING OR ONE-OFF: Permanent

SIZE (METRES OR FEET): 15 m × 6 m × 3.3 m

DESIGNER: John Dangerfield Associates, London, England as consultants to Jasper Jacob Associates

BRIEF: To recreate a section of a fire trench on the Somme towards the end of 1916 which would graphically communicate to the visitor the conditions endured by front-line troops and the routine which governed their days; to illustrate various components of the trench system such as dug-outs, fire bays, regimental aid posts etc.

ATTENDANCE: Public

This exhibit achieves high standards of authenticity within the constraints of the space available – whereas smoke and gunfire can be simulated, mud and the appalling smell of the trench system can only be suggested.

Imperial War Museum

PROJECT: The Blitz Experience

DATE AND LOCATION: 1989, The Imperial War Museum, London, England

PERMANENT, TRAVELLING OR ONE-OFF: Permanent

SIZE (METRES OR FEET): 15 m × 6 m × 3.3 m

DESIGNER: John Dangerfield Associates, London, England as a consultant to Jasper Jacob Associates

BRIEF: To recreate a small part of a street in the East End of London during the height of the blitz in autumn 1940; to provide a visual and aural experience for parties of 15 to 20 visitors.

ATTENDANCE: Public

Vibrating floors, smoke and moving elements in the set engage the visitors' senses and help to produce an authentic 'experience'.

Imperial War Museum

PROJECT: Belsen 1945

DATE AND LOCATION: 1991, The Imperial War
Museum, London, England

PERMANENT, TRAVELLING OR ONE-OFF: Permanent

SIZE (METRES OR FEET): 7.25 m × 6.65 m × 2.4 m

DESIGNER: John Dangerfield Associates, London,
England; graphics: IWM Exhibition Department

BRIEF: To commemorate the liberation of the
concentration camp at Bergen-Belsen by the British
Army in April 1945; to display film and photographic
archive taken by British Army cameraman and
photographers now in the collection of the Imperial
War Museum.

ATTENDANCE: Public

A suitably simple, even austere system of black and
white and grey panels, drained of all colour except
for the dramatic swastika panel, which
incorporates part of a flag found at the camp.
A sense of cruelty and disorientation is created
without the physical replication of a concentration
camp; fibre optic lighting emphasizes the coldness
of the interior.

The Jerusalem Foundation

PROJECT: 3000 years of the history of the City
of Jerusalem

DATE AND LOCATION: 1989, Tower of David
Musuem, The Citadel, Jerusalem, Israel

PERMANENT, TRAVELLING OR ONE-OFF: Permanent

SIZE (METRES OR FEET): 2800 sq m

DESIGNER: James Gardner (3D Concepts) Ltd,
London, England

BRIEF: To relate the history of Jerusalem,
emphasizing its significance to the three major
faiths: Judaism, Christianity and Islam, Purpose-
made reconstructions and replicas bring past
situations alive in a walk-through history

ATTENDANCE: Public

This spectacularly curved relief wall shows the
Jewish return to Jerusalem from exile in Babylon,
executed in the manner of the period. The original
was modelled in clay, then cast in GRP impregnated
with marble dust.

National Museum of Science

PROJECT: Evolution of Life from its Origins to Modern Man

DATE AND LOCATION: 1988, Taichung, Taiwan, ROC

PERMANENT, TRAVELLING OR ONE-OFF: Permanent

SIZE (METRES OR FEET): 8500 sq m

DESIGNER: James Gardner (3D Concepts) Ltd, London, England

BRIEF: Ten linked galleries sequentially relate the natural sciences from the origins of life to modern man. Separate galleries off the main route are devoted to the human body, colour in nature, numbers and forms in nature and sounds in nature. A living arboretum extension shows the evolution of plant life.

ATTENDANCE: Public

In this section illustrating the development of life in the seas, engravings of soft-bodied creatures are appropriately etched on edge-lit plexiglass. Overhead looms one of nature's most ferocious creatures, a giant sea scorpion.

Victoria and Albert Museum

PROJECT: The Tsui Gallery of Chinese Art

DATE AND LOCATION: June 1991, Victoria and Albert Museum, London, England

PERMANENT, TRAVELLING OR ONE-OFF: Permanent

SIZE (METRES OR FEET): 612 sq m

DESIGNER: Fitch RS, London, England

BRIEF: To create a permanent, controlled environment for the Museum's Chinese collections which will demystify Chinese art and culture and stimulate the maximum degree of public interest in China.

ATTENDANCE: Public

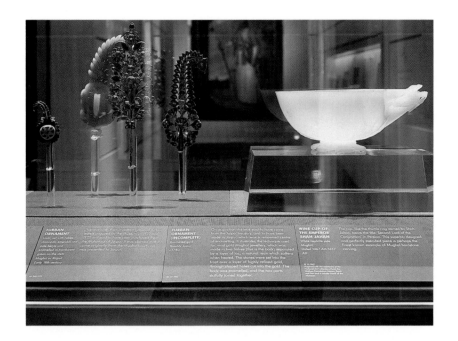

Victoria and Albert Museum

PROJECT: Nehru Gallery of Indian Art, 1750–1900

DATE AND LOCATION: November 1990, Victoria and Albert Museum, London, England

PERMANENT, TRAVELLING OR ONE-OFF: Permanent

SIZE (METRES OR FEET): 450 sq m

DESIGNER: Brian Griggs, Head of Design, Victoria and Albert Museum Design Department and Tim Molloy

BRIEF: To create a setting based on a Mogul Court during the period of the Mogul Empire (1526–1875).

ATTENDANCE: Public

The main feature is a 17th-century colonnade from Ajmer in the Rajasthan region, which leads to a central raised pavilion in which art from the Mogul Court is displayed. The design uses traditional Indian materials to form the setting.

The British Museum

PROJECT: Madagascar, Island of the Ancestors

DATE AND LOCATION: 1987–89, Museum of
Mankind, London, England

PERMANENT, TRAVELLING OR ONE-OFF: Temporary

SIZE (METRES OR FEET): 549 sq m

DESIGNER: British Museum Design Office, London,
England

BRIEF: To evoke the history and quality of life on
Madagascar

ATTENDANCE: Public

The effect of this richly evocative reconstruction
of village life is enhanced by the dramatic
spotlighting.

Photography courtesy of the Trustees of the British Museum.

Mobil Oil

PROJECT: Treasures of Ancient Nigeria

DATE AND LOCATION: 1982, Royal Academy, London

PERMANENT, TRAVELLING OR ONE-OFF: Travelling

SIZE (METRES OR FEET): 700 sq m

DESIGNER: Alan Irvine Architect, London, England

BRIEF: To demonstrate the richness of Nigeria's artistic heritage in bronze, stone and clay sculptures dating from the first millenium BC to the second millenium AD, the high point being the magnificent group of Benin bronzes. The works were shown in frameless perspex cases in a series of darkened rooms, with the visitors' route being indicated by a central path of contrasted flooring.

ATTENDANCE: Public

A masterful use of lighting to create dramatic effect.

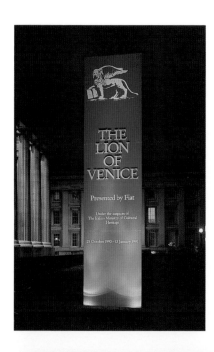

Fiat

PROJECT : The Lion of Venice

DATE AND LOCATION : 1991, The British Museum, London, England

PERMANENT, TRAVELLING OR ONE-OFF : One-off

SIZE (METRES OR FEET) : Spread over gallery and staircase

DESIGNER : Alan Irvine Architect, London, England

BRIEF : To exhibit the bronze lion of Venice before its restitution.

ATTENDANCE : Public

The great bronze lion of Venice, symbol of the city-state, was taken down from its column in the Piazzetta for examination and restoration. Before being replaced it was exhibited in Amsterdam and London with related exhibits showing its stylistic origins and its place in the history of the city. The Lion was placed on a two-metre high plinth at the foot of the main staircase in the entrance hall of the British Museum and the related material, included paintings by Bellini and Carpaccio, was shown in a specially designed room.

Glass of the Caesars continued over page

Olivetti

PROJECT: The Glass of the Caesars

DATE AND LOCATION: 1987, The British Museum, London, England

PERMANENT, TRAVELLING OR ONE-OFF: Travelling (London, Cologne, Rome)

SIZE (METRES OR FEET): 500 sq m

DESIGNER: Alan Irvine Architect, London, England

BRIEF: To display 160 pieces of the finest Roman glass in a highly secure yet portable exhibition. Specifically designed, high-security conservation level cases constructed of non-reflective glass were commissioned. The lighting was adjustable (tungsten halogen spotlights fixed above each case). The cases were demountable to pack flat for transportation to the three locations.

ATTENDANCE: Public

34

Glass of the Caesars

The exhibition probably looked its best here, in the
Capitoline Museum, Rome, Italy, where it was
shown in 1988.

The Royal Academy

PROJECT: The Great Japan Exhibition: Art of the Edo Period 1600–1868

DATE AND LOCATION: 1983, Royal Academy, London, England

PERMANENT, TRAVELLING OR ONE-OFF: One-off

SIZE (METRES OR FEET): 2000 sq m

DESIGNER: Alan Irvine Architect, London, England and Kisho Kurakawa, Tokyo, Japan

BRIEF: To display exhibits of screens, calligraphy, lacquer, sculpture, ceramics, kimonos, armour etc including National Treasures. The design of the exhibition was Japanese in character, using simple and elegant materials, many of which were brought from Japan. The rooms were generally arranged in chronological sequence with special displays devoted to specific items.

ATTENDANCE: Public

The British Museum

PROJECT: Urasenke Tea House, Urasenke Gallery

DATE AND LOCATION: 1990, British Museum,
London, England

PERMANENT, TRAVELLING OR ONE-OFF: Permanent

SIZE (METRES OR FEET): 15 sq m (gallery);
3 m (height) × 3 m (width) × 2.5 m (depth)
for teahouse

DESIGNER: British Museum Design Office, London,
England

BRIEF: To provide a Japanese tea house for
permanent display

ATTENDANCE: Public

Photography courtesy of the Trustees of the British Museum.

The Queen's House, Greenwich

PROJECT: Entrance archway (Inigo Jones 1614) with view through to exhibition chambers

DATE AND LOCATION: 1990, grounds of the National Maritime Museum, Greenwich, London, England

PERMANENT, TRAVELLING OR ONE-OFF: Permanent

SIZE (METRES OR FEET): 250 sq m

DESIGNER: John Ronayne, Ronayne Design, London, England

BRIEF: To convert the undercroft of The Queen's House (by Inigo Jones for the queen of James I) into a permanent exhibition about the architecture and history of the house, including a treasury for secure showcase display of the Museum's collection of gold and silver.

ATTENDANCE: Public

The information panels, with backlit graphics, are custom made in steel. General lighting comes from fibre-optics in the floor.

Tate Gallery

PROJECT: The Age of Charles I

DATE AND LOCATION: 1973, The Tate Gallery, London, England

PERMANENT, TRAVELLING OR ONE-OFF: One-off

SIZE (METRES OR FEET): 1500 sq m

DESIGNER: Alan Irvine Architect, London, England

BRIEF: To demonstrate the principal tendencies in English painting between the middle years of James I and the execution of his son, Charles I, in 1649. The majority of the exhibits came from the Royal Collection and included paintings, drawings, sculpture, models and miniatures.

ATTENDANCE: Public

The Geffrye Museum

PROJECT: 'Putting on the Style: Setting up Home in the 1950s'. Popular domestic interior style in postwar England.

DATE AND LOCATION: 1990, London, England

PERMANENT, TRAVELLING OR ONE-OFF: Temporary, but two of the five reconstructed rooms were retained to form the basis of two new permanent period room displays.

SIZE (METRES OR FEET): 54 sq m × 2 (upper and lower galleries)

DESIGNER: Graham Simpson, Simpson Molloy, London, England

BRIEF: To design an appropriate shell for five reconstructed 1950s rooms, ranging from an architect's living room to a bed-sit, plus graphic panels. The exhibition examined the contemporary influences and aspirations in the choice of furniture and interior decor, based on original research with reference to design, social and oral histories. The rooms were dressed by the client with furniture and artefacts from the Museum's collection and from lenders. The shell had to create an overall 1950s look without distracting the spectator from the room sets themselves.

ATTENDANCE: Public

National Museum of Photography, Film and Television

PROJECT: Film and Television in Society

DATE AND LOCATION: 1986, National Museum of Photography, Film and Television, Bradford, Yorkshire, England

PERMANENT, TRAVELLING OR ONE-OFF: Permanent

SIZE (METRES OR FEET): 10 sq ft

DESIGNER: National Gallery of Photography, Film and Television Design

BRIEF: To recreate an image of the impact of television on the family life of the 1930s

ATTENDANCE: Public

Mannequins and models are difficult to use well in static displays, but here the effect is necessary and successful, mainly because of the realistic poses and the strong lighting on their faces 'seemingly' coming from the TV screen.

California Wine Patrons

PROJECT: California Wine: The Science of an Art

DATE AND LOCATION: 1989, Californian Museum of Science and Industry, Los Angeles, California, USA

PERMANENT, TRAVELLING OR ONE-OFF: Permanent

SIZE (METRES OR FEET): 2500 sq ft

DESIGNER: Louis Nelson Associates Inc, New York City, New York, USA

BRIEF: To present information about the interplay of science and art in wine production and the effect of alcohol on the body and human behaviour

ATTENDANCE: Public, wine trade

The stainless steel floor, ceiling and cylinders (reminiscent of wine vats) are the primary surfaces and reflect the computerized environment and colour changes. Graphic walls are backlit films with transparencies, video monitors and touch screens incorporated. Three dimensional models and games protrude from the walls. The exhibition is bathed in an ever changing array of coloured light adding the dimension of time.

45

Franklin Science Museum (Future Center)

PROJECT: Home, Future Home

DATE AND LOCATION: 1990, Franklin Science
Museum, Philadelphia, Pennsylvania, USA

PERMANENT, TRAVELLING OR ONE-OFF: Permanent

SIZE (METRES OR FEET): 400 sq feet

DESIGNER: Ricardo Morin/Design Etc. Inc, New York
City, New York, USA

BRIEF: To humanize the face of future technology,
in particular how technology affects the arts, our
daily lives and home design.

ATTENDANCE: Public

La Villette

PROJECT: La Cité-Ciné

DATE AND LOCATION: January 1987 to February
1988, Parc de la Villette, Paris, France

PERMANENT, TRAVELLING OR ONE-OFF: One-off

SIZE (METRES OR FEET): 8000 sq m

DESIGNER: François Confino

BRIEF: To bring together the city in terms of the
cinema.

ATTENDANCE: Public

Within this vast iron hall, every aspect of cinema
was recreated, from a 'street' of movie sets in
which scenes from each movie 'type' were shown,
to a section of the Paris metro line at the end of
which a cinema screen showed underground clips.

La Villette

PROJECT: La Cité-Ciné

DATE AND LOCATION: January 1987 to February
1988, Parc de la Villette, Paris, France

PERMANENT, TRAVELLING OR ONE-OFF: One-off

SIZE (METRES OR FEET): 8000 sq m

DESIGNER: François Confino

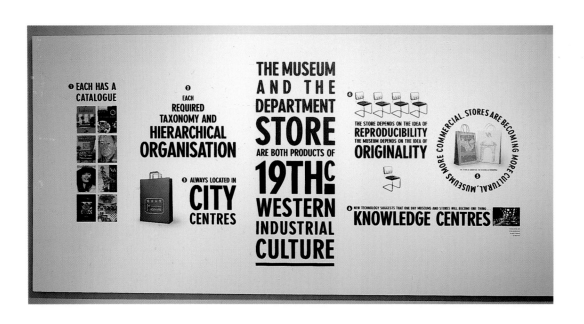

Iowa Rural Electric Cooperative

PROJECT: Iowa REC Power House

DATE AND LOCATION: August 1989, Iowa State Fair, Iowa, USA

PERMANENT, TRAVELLING OR ONE-OFF: One-off

SIZE (METRES OR FEET): 578 sq ft

DESIGNER: John Sayles, Sayles Graphics, Des Moines, Iowa, USA

BRIEF: To show the impact of electricity in everyday life using graphic oversized appliances made from wood and accented with neon.

ATTENDANCE: Public

GOT THE BEAT

DOWN ON

GREEK STREET

Drake University, Des Moines, Iowa, USA

PROJECT: 'We've got the beat down on Greek
Street'

DATE AND LOCATION: June 1990, Drake University,
Des Moines, Iowa, USA

PERMANENT, TRAVELLING OR ONE-OFF: One-off

SIZE (METRES OR FEET): 96 sq ft

DESIGNER: John Sayles, Sayles Graphic Design,
Des Moines, Iowa, USA

BRIEF: To attract the freshman students at Drake
University so they would sign up to participate in
fraternity and sorority (Greek) week. The exhibition
was part of a promotional campaign which
included posters, mailings and sportswear.

ATTENDANCE: Freshman students

San Francisco Zoological Society

PROJECT: Primate Discovery Center

DATE AND LOCATION: 1985, San Francisco Zoo, San Francisco, California, USA

PERMANENT, TRAVELLING OR ONE-OFF: Permanent

SIZE (METRES OR FEET): 148 sq m

DESIGNER: The Burdick Group, San Francisco, California, USA

BRIEF: To create an 'information-rich zoo' in which animals are organized by what can be learned from them. Animals are clustered around Discovery Centers featuring participatory exhibits that stimulate visitor involvement. Animal signage alerts visitors on specific traits when viewing live animals.

ATTENDANCE: Public

**The 1983 Brooklyn Bridge Centennial
Commission**

PROJECT: 'Anatomy of the Bridge', a celebratory
exhibition about the building of the Brooklyn
Bridge

DATE AND LOCATION: May to November 1989,
The Anchorage, Brooklyn, New York, USA

PERMANENT, TRAVELLING OR ONE-OFF: One-off

SIZE (METRES OR FEET): 5000 sq m

DESIGNER: Keith Godard/StudioWorks*, New York
City, New York, USA; fabricator: Jim Mellor and
Crawford Studios

BRIEF: To describe the building of the bridge in
terms understandable to people without an
engineering background.

ATTENDANCE: Public

The New York Landmarks Conservancy

PROJECT: 'The Palace of Commerce', an exhibit that tells the story of the Beaux-Arts Building and proposals for its future usage.

DATE AND LOCATION: November 1983 to August 1991, US Customs House, New York City, New York, USA

PERMANENT, TRAVELLING OR ONE-OFF: One-off

SIZE (METRES OR FEET): 316 sq ft

DESIGNER: Keith Godard/StudioWorks*, New York City, New York, USA; fabricator: Gary Faro/ Wayne Walker

BRIEF: To raise public concern regarding the future of the turn-of-the-century US Customs building, which had been closed for some time; to lobby for its preservation by demonstrating alternative usages.

ATTENDANCE: Public

The exhibit's graphics were mounted on 16 glass panels to give information about the original architectural competition and the history of Lower Manhattan. The site became so popular that it became an established local rendezvous – a landmark in itself.

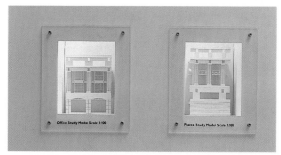

Paternoster Exhibition

PROJECT: Proposed development at the Paternoster site adjacent to St Paul's Cathedral

DATE AND LOCATION: 1989, The Crypt, St Paul's Cathedral, London, England

PERMANENT, TRAVELLING OR ONE-OFF: One-off

SIZE (METRES OR FEET): 90 sq m

DESIGNER: Williams & Phoa, London, England

BRIEF: To work with the architects Arup Associates to design an exhibition that would explain the intricacies of the development while being sympathetic to the Crypt of St Paul's.

ATTENDANCE: Public

How refreshing to see a simple, understated format, using pale materials and neatly integrating the lighting so that there is no conflict with the beautifully arched ceiling.

Winchester Cathedral

PROJECT: Winchester Cathedral Treasury

DATE AND LOCATION: 1971, Winchester Cathedral, Winchester, Hampshire, England

PERMANENT, TRAVELLING OR ONE-OFF: Permanent

SIZE (METRES OR FEET): Upper level of Cathedral

DESIGNER: Alan Irvine Architect, London, England

BRIEF: To show the silver plate used in the Cathedral ceremonies and similar items from local churches, previously kept in high security conditions and not seen by the public except when in use. The site is approached via a small circular staircase to an upper level in the transept of the cathedral. The glazed central showcase, which has a transparent top, is lit externally from a chandelier suspended above. The profile of the case enables the silver to be seen from different viewpoints and levels. The materials used are bronze, marble and rare woods.

ATTENDANCE: Public

Lloyds Museum of London

PROJECT: The Lloyds Image

DATE AND LOCATION: October 1989, Lloyds
Building, London, England

PERMANENT, TRAVELLING OR ONE-OFF: Permanent

SIZE (METRES OR FEET): 1190 sq m

DESIGNER: John Hart Design Consultants,
Guildford, Surrey, England; construction: Central
Display Productions, London, England

BRIEF: To project a positive image of the Lloyds of
today, the future and beyond.

ATTENDANCE: Lloyds personnel and visitors

Housed within the famous Richard Rogers building,
this simple display takes a lively, appropriately
high-tech approach to a potentially boring subject.

York Archaeology Trust

PROJECT: Jorvik Viking Centre

DATE AND LOCATION: April 1984, Jorvik Viking Centre, York, Yorkshire, England

PERMANENT, TRAVELLING OR ONE-OFF: Permanent

SIZE (METRES OR FEET): 1500 sq m (reconstruction area)

DESIGNER: John Sunderland Design, Allerston, Pickering, North Yorkshire, England

BRIEF: To recreate part of Viking York on the site of the archaeological dig; to entertain and educate the public about life in Viking times.

ATTENDANCE: Public

This display was one of the pioneers in the UK of this type of exhibit, involving as it does the senses of smell and touch as well as the visual and taking the visitor physically through a set of experiences, in the way that Disney and the old-fashioned ghost train once did.

Carlisle City Council

PROJECT: Tullie House Museum

DATE AND LOCATION: May 1991, Tullie House Museum, Carlisle, Cumbria, England

PERMANENT, TRAVELLING OR ONE-OFF: Permanent

SIZE (METRES OR FEET): 1200 sq m

DESIGNER: John Ronayne Design, London, England

BRIEF: To devise, design and supervise construction of new permanent £1 million display on the theme of Carlisle's historic border location

ATTENDANCE: Public

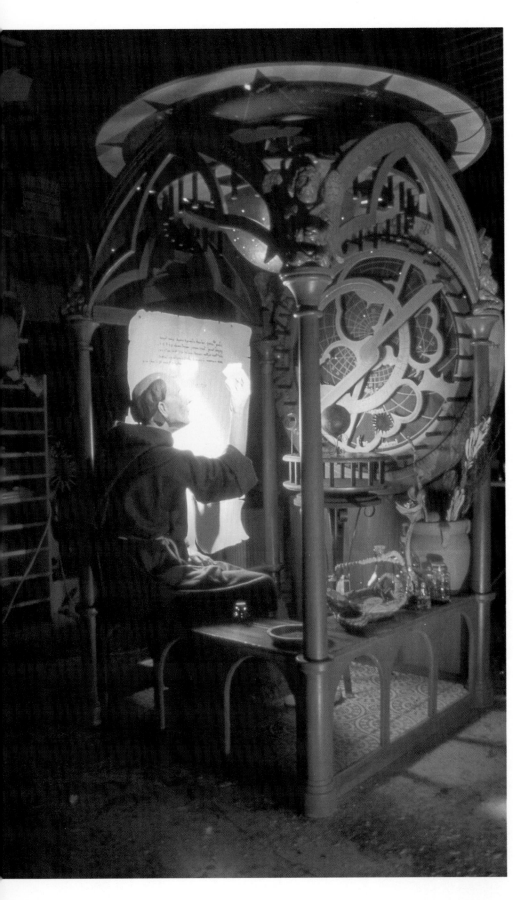

The Oxford Story

PROJECT: Roger Bacon

DATE AND LOCATION: May 1990, Oxford Visitor
Centre, Oxford, Oxfordshire, England

PERMANENT, TRAVELLING OR ONE-OFF: Permanent

SIZE (METRES OR FEET): 2.25 sq m

DESIGNER: N. J. Farmer Studios, Leicester, England

BRIEF: To 'bring to life' Roger Bacon, the 12th
century Oxford philosopher who had a consuming
interest in mathematics, astronomy, lenses and
prisms, chemistry, physics and natural sciences.
The tableau vivant demonstrates the passions of his
life, combining scientific artefacts within a gothic
arched frame symbolizing a monk's cell. An
intricate system of gears and cogs turn a giant
astrolabe, an orrery and a pierced copper dome
which projects stars and moons around the room.

ATTENDANCE: Public

This evocative display illustrates how much
atmosphere and detail can be created within a
tiny space.

Selkirk Museum Service

PROJECT: Recreation of 19th-century ironmongery shop

DATE AND LOCATION: 1984, Halliwells House, Selkirk, Borders, Scotland

PERMANENT, TRAVELLING OR ONE-OFF: Permanent

SIZE (METRES OR FEET): 45 sq m

DESIGNER: Jim Clark Design, South Queensferry, Scotland

BRIEF: To recreate social life in and around Selkirk; this is one of six such units housed in a listed building that was once itself an ironmongery shop.

ATTENDANCE: Public

Everyone is fascinated by this type of exhibit, seeming to take us back in time to a childhood we hardly remember or, in some cases, never knew. Britain has many examples of this 'recreated' shop, but it is equally popular now in America, Japan and Australia. These same elements are what retailers such as Ralph Lauren have adopted to enrich their shopping experience.

Wiltshire Archaeological and Natural History Society

PROJECT: Museum Gallery of Social History

DATE AND LOCATION: 1988, Devizes Museum, Devizes, Wiltshire, England

PERMANENT, TRAVELLING OR ONE-OFF: Permanent

SIZE (METRES OR FEET): 68 sq m

DESIGNER: Bremner & Orr Design Consultants, Tetbury, Gloucestershire, England

BRIEF: To produce an integrated display of original fittings and artefacts and supportive graphics, including opportunities for role-play by visiting groups; a 'magazine' approach to a diverse collection of social history.

ATTENDANCE: Public

Hull Borough Council

PROJECT: School Days. The history of school from the 12th century to the present day

DATE AND LOCATION: 1988/9, The Old Grammar School, Hull, Yorkshire, England

PERMANENT, TRAVELLING OR ONE-OFF: Temporary

SIZE (METRES OR FEET): 236 sq m

DESIGNER: HRA, Chester, Cheshire, England

BRIEF: To design and supervise the internal conversion of a 16th century grammar school into an exhibition centre; to create the first of a series of temporary exhibitions on the ground floor, including exhibition systems for continuing use; to design and install a permanent display on the first floor dealing with the lives of Hull people throughout the centuries.

ATTENDANCE: Public

Hull Borough Council

PROJECT: Street Life: The History of Transport in
the borough of Kingston upon Hull

DATE AND LOCATION: 1990, Hull Museum of
Transport, Hull, Yorkshire, England

PERMANENT, TRAVELLING OR ONE-OFF: Permanent

SIZE (METRES OR FEET): 514 sq m

DESIGNER: HRA, Chester, Cheshire, England

BRIEF: To make an exciting and unusual exhibition
about the impact of technological change on social
life in the borough; to display some of the
Museum's collection of large objects in a manner
appealing to the widest audience, especially school
students.

ATTENDANCE: Public

English Heritage

PROJECT: Portchester Castle

DATE AND LOCATION: 1990, Portsmouth Harbour, Portsmouth, Hampshire, England

PERMANENT, TRAVELLING OR ONE-OFF: Permanent

DESIGNER: John Furneaux and Laurie Stewart/ Furneaux Stewart, London, England

BRIEF: To design a permanent interpretative exhibition covering Portchester's Roman origins through Saxon and medieval periods to the present day. The exhibition is housed within the two basement rooms of the keep. Display techniques are designed to incorporate, where appropriate, artefacts, interactive displays and illustrations pertinent to the particular subject. Large blocks of text and separate showcases have been avoided.

ATTENDANCE: Public

**Royal Northumberland Fusiliers
Regimental Museum**

PROJECT: The Fighting Fifth

DATE AND LOCATION: May 1990, The Abbot's
Tower, Alnwick Castle, Alnwick, Northumberland,
England

PERMANENT, TRAVELLING OR ONE-OFF: Permanent

SIZE (METRES OR FEET): 38.25 sq m

DESIGNER: John Furneaux and Laurie Stewart/
Furneaux Stewart, London, England

BRIEF: To present the story of the Regiment from
1674 to 1963 from the soldier's point of view,
using letters, diaries and personal items of
equipment. Subjects covered: Origins, Recruitment
and Training; Campaigns; Wives and Sweethearts;
Prisoners of War; Sport and Leisure; Our Regiment.

ATTENDANCE: Public

This exhibit echoes the vaulted space it inhabits by
using curved panels and an arched lighting system.

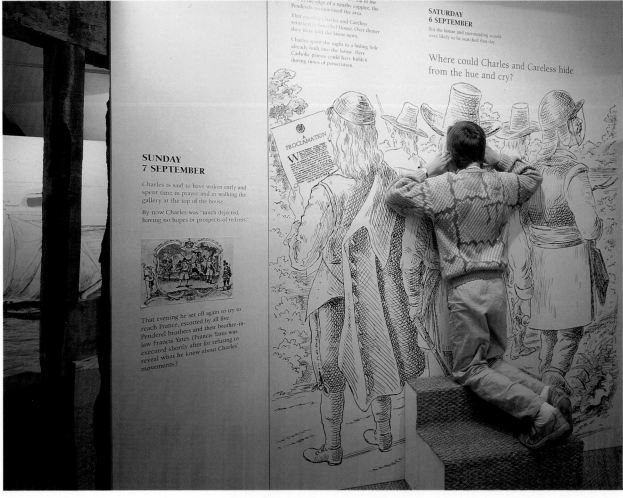

Travelling Exhibitions The

requirements of an exhibition that has to withstand the rigours of being dismantled, packed up, transported and reassembled not once but many times are considerable. The layout of the show often needs to be adapted to fit different configuarations in a variety of venues and to break down again into small components for storage. In addition some exhibitions need to be free-standing and include the structure in which they are housed.

The Arts Council of Great Britain
PROJECT: Read All About It
DATE AND LOCATION: March 1990 and ongoing;
touring British libraries nationwide
PERMANENT, TRAVELLING OR ONE-OFF: Travelling
SIZE (METRES OR FEET): 16.8 sq m
DESIGNER: Neil Smith/Giant Limited, London,
England
BRIEF: To produce five exhibition systems within a
£20,000 budget; they had to be portable, durable
and easily assembled. The graphics on the panels
had to be lively, as the purpose was to encourage
library-users to read more widely and try their hand
at creative writing.
ATTENDANCE: Public

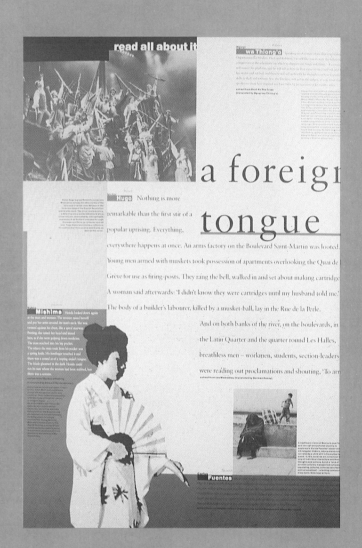

Fundacio 'Caixa de Pensions' – Museo de la Ciencia de Barcelona

PROJECT: La Carpa de la Ciencia
DATE AND LOCATION: 1991, touring Spain
PERMANENT, TRAVELLING OR ONE-OFF: Travelling
SIZE (METRES OR FEET): 550 sq m
DESIGNER: Carlos Rolando, Rosalia Ferrando/CR
Communications and Design SA, Barcelona, Spain;
construction: Quod, Barcelona, Spain
BRIEF: To create a 'travelling circus', an offshoot
of the Science Museum, which includes basic
characteristics: experimentation workshops, films,
lectures etc. to show and teach a young audience
how interesting science can be.
ATTENDANCE: Public (school pupils)

Like a circus, this exhibit travels the country in
trucks, spending just over a month in each of the
towns it visits.

The Crafts Council

PROJECT: New Spirit in Craft and Design

DATE AND LOCATION: 1987-88, touring UK for 16 months

PERMANENT, TRAVELLING OR ONE-OFF: Travelling

SIZE (METRES OR FEET): 18 000 sq ft

DESIGNER: John Kember and Meredith Bowles/The Finsbury Plan, London, England

BRIEF: To design an exhibition to showcase the work of new and young craftspeople. Many skills were exhibited, from neon and jewellery to metal and textiles, creating a great challenge to display.

ATTENDANCE: Public

This exhibit, photographed at the Crafts Council Gallery, Waterloo Place, London, England, is Neon Lights by Peter Freeman.

Canary Wharf/Olympia and York

PROJECT: The Green and Open Spaces of Canary Wharf

DATE AND LOCATION: 1990, Chelsea Flower Show

PERMANENT, TRAVELLING OR ONE-OFF: One-off

SIZE (METRES OR FEET): 100 sq m

DESIGNER: Flashman Associates, London, England; graphics: Williams and Phoa, London, England

BRIEF: To convey the verdant nature of the open spaces at Canary Wharf which was planted to look good throughout the year. Close up images of shrubs were used as a backdrop to indicative photographs and drawings.

ATTENDANCE: Public and trade

Shell International

PROJECT: The coordination of Shell's five company divisions

DATE AND LOCATION: June 1991, The Royal Show, Stoneleigh, Warwickshire, England

PERMANENT, TRAVELLING OR ONE-OFF: Annual

SIZE (METRES OR FEET): 80 sq m

DESIGNER: Philip Wong/Carter Wong, London, England

BRIEF: To create an exhibition which showed the five different divisions of the group (indicated by the banners) coordinated as one. Each division was illustrated by drawing parallels with nature and wildlife: Resources is equated with a bird, Innovation with a bee and so forth. Columns and methods of display were kept simple and uncluttered.

ATTENDANCE: Trade

Simple white panels are held by tension cables from metal rods at the top so that nothing conflicts with the graphics. The illustrations (far left) by Brian Cook evoke the 1930s.

Dow Plastics

PROJECT: Plastics recycling

DATE AND LOCATION: June 1990; displayed in shopping malls and museums of science and industry throughout USA

PERMANENT, TRAVELLING OR ONE-OFF: Travelling

SIZE (METRES OR FEET): 93 sq m

DESIGNER: The Burdick Group, San Francisco, California, USA

BRIEF: To present plastic recycling information in an engaging and visually exciting way. Interactive exhibit elements on wheels link together to form a 'Plastics Train' designed to roll from transport truck to exhibit space.

ATTENDANCE: Public

Westfield Inc

PROJECT: Shopping Center Development and
Leasing

DATE AND LOCATION: First use in 1988,
International Council of Shopping Centers' Leasing
Mall, Las Vegas, Nevada, USA

PERMANENT, TRAVELLING OR ONE-OFF: Travelling

SIZE (METRES OR FEET): 1152 sq ft

DESIGNER: Josh Freeman Associates, Los Angeles,
California, USA

BRIEF: To reconfigure an existing system of
structural components to maximize visibility and
breathe new life into the corporate presentation of
Westfield Inc, an American company with
Austrialian roots which owns shopping centers
throughout the USA.

ATTENDANCE: Public

Citizen Europe Ltd

PROJECT: Computer Exhibit

DATE AND LOCATION: March 1990, CeBit, Hanover, Germany

PERMANENT, TRAVELLING OR ONE-OFF: Travelling (also exhibited in Birmingham, Paris, Milan and Munich)

SIZE (METRES OR FEET): 290 sq m

DESIGNER: Dave Hobday and Steve Gordon/Dave Hobday Design, London, England; contractor: Design and Constructing Services

BRIEF: To display the client's range of computers and printers. The stand had to be designed like robust, pre-wired Lego that could easily be built, dismantled and rebuilt with the minimum damage, labour and transport.

ATTENDANCE: Computer trade, public

Modular, kitform and self assembly

Ready-made systems can often be adapted or customized to suit individual requirements, but designers often prefer to produce their own tailor-made structure. The choice of materials may need to reflect the client's image; and if the show has to stay up for a long time cleaning and durability will be important. Some exhibitions need to include their own lighting as well as shelves, display cases, leaflet dispensers and even audio-visual equipment.

Simpson Paper Company

PROJECT: Annual Printed Papers Competition

DATE AND LOCATION: A travelling exhibition making 30–40 visits a year

PERMANENT, TRAVELLING OR ONE-OFF: Travelling

SIZE (METRES OR FEET): 16 modules 2 ft × 2 ft × 5 ft which can be arranged to fit any floor plan

DESIGNER: T. Wayne Hunt and Katherine Go/Wayne Hunt Design Inc, Pasadena, California, USA

BRIEF: To provide a lightweight, re-usable travelling exhibition of Simpson Paper Competition winners. Designed so that one person can set it up, host a reception, de-mount and repack in three hours. A neutral field was provided for art display with 'architectural' details for visual interest.

ATTENDANCE: Trade

A wonderfully simple system of individual panels and chunky, pyramid-shaped bases.

McNaughton Paper

PROJECT: Exhibition Stand promoting two
McNaughton paper ranges

DATE AND LOCATION: October 1990, National
Graphics Exhibition, London, England

PERMANENT, TRAVELLING OR ONE-OFF: Travelling

SIZE (METRES OR FEET): 5 stands 2 m × 750 mm

DESIGNER: David Pocknell, Paul Sheridan/Pocknell
and Green, Wethersfield, Essex, England

BRIEF: To design a portable knock-down flexible
exhibition system that could be easily transported
and installed by one person.

ATTENDANCE: Trade

The British Council

PROJECT: Pop! British music in the 1980s

DATE AND LOCATION: A five-year exhibition travelling worldwide (Africa, Eastern Europe, Scandinavia, India etc)

PERMANENT, TRAVELLING OR ONE-OFF: Travelling

SIZE (METRES OR FEET): 60 sets of three panels, each panel 594 mm × 422 mm

DESIGNER: structure: Jiricna Kerr Associates, London, England; graphics: The Partners Design Consultants Ltd, London, England

BRIEF: To make the point that many pop stars are British, although America is assumed to monopolise the industry; to design a flexible, sturdy yet lightweight display that would be easy to assemble and dismantle and be able to accommodate itself to the different spaces and venues it would be shown in; to make it easy to update to reflect current pop trends.

ATTENDANCE: Public

The British Council

PROJECT: All Dressed Up: British Fashion in the 1980s

DATE AND LOCATION: Preview at the Royal College of Art, London, England, July 1988; then a long-term tour of Eastern bloc countries

PERMANENT, TRAVELLING OR ONE-OFF: Travelling

SIZE (METRES OR FEET): 40 modules of 4 sq ft each when assembled

DESIGNER: Neil Cavagan and Joseph Mitchell/ Platform Design, London, England

BRIEF: To produce a simple, self-explanatory exhibition 'kit', lightweight and low cost, that could easily be packed up for transport; complicated fittings and fixings were avoided, as were lighting and electrical systems.

ATTENDANCE: Public

A curious combination of high and low level panels, shelves, showcases and decorative metal endpanels that form an interesting and lively island unit.

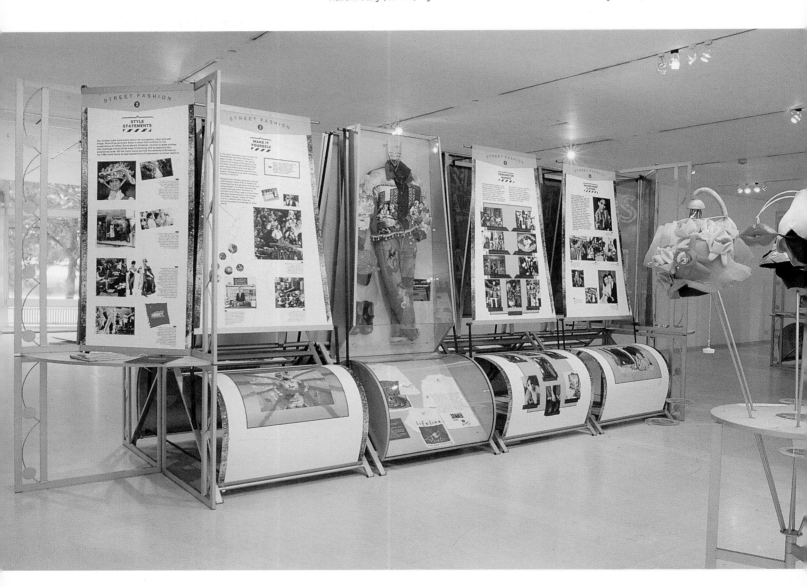

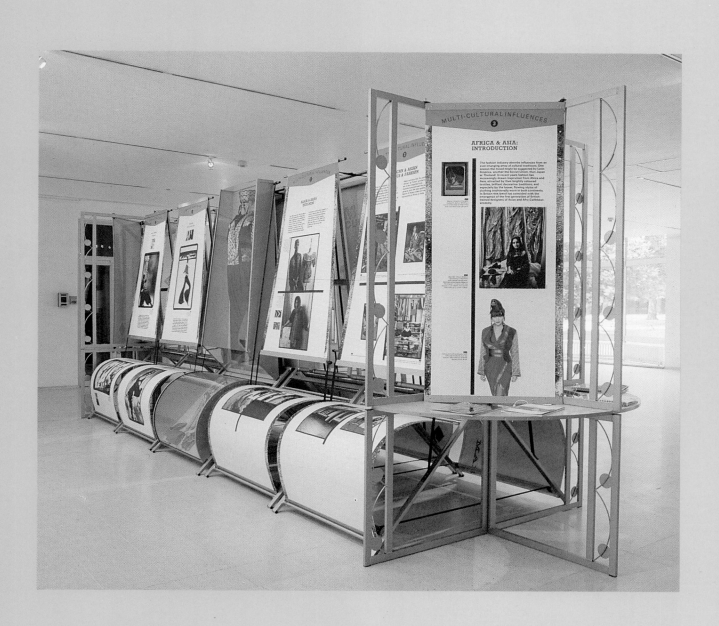

The Design Museum

PROJECT: Launch of book on corporate identity

DATE AND LOCATION: November 1989, The Design Museum, London, England

PERMANENT, TRAVELLING OR ONE-OFF: One-off

SIZE (METRES OR FEET): 50 sq ft

DESIGNER: Sir Terence Conran, RSCG Conran, London, England; graphics: Alison Tomlin/Carter Wong, London, England.

BRIEF: To design a coherent exhibition for the launch of a new book. The solution was to use single artists' easels with single boards on each; these were designed using simple images from the book, displayed in a graphic manner.

ATTENDANCE: Public

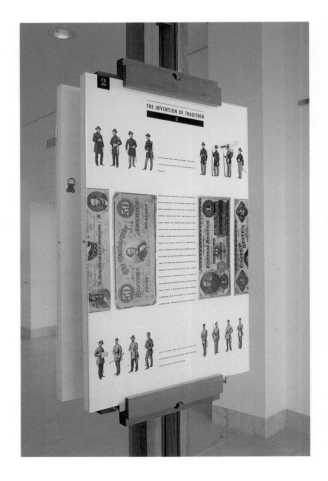

Friends of the Earth

PROJECT: Friends of the Earth flagship exhibition

DATE AND LOCATION: First shown at the Labour
Party Conference, September 1990

PERMANENT, TRAVELLING OR ONE-OFF: Travelling

SIZE (METRES OR FEET): Basic plan 2 sq m or 3 sq m
depending on configuration

DESIGNER: The Association of Ideas, London,
England

BRIEF: To create a transportable, flexible
lightweight exhibition system for environmentally-
friendly, recycled or recyclable materials; to raise
the image of the organization by establishing a
professional' image to communicate precise and
accurate messages.

ATTENDANCE: Public

A very animated system that provides wide and
narrow panels, directional spots and atmospheric
uplighting and even a handy literature dispenser.

The New York Landmarks Conservancy

PROJECT: 'Preserving Sacred Sites in the Empire State'. Exhibit displaying religious properties in New York State.

DATE AND LOCATION: April 1989, The Municipal Art Society, New York City, New York, USA

PERMANENT, TRAVELLING OR ONE-OFF: Travelling

SIZE (METRES OR FEET): Three modules 10 ft high × 5 ft wide

DESIGNER: Keith Godard/StudioWorks*, New York City, New York, USA; fabricator: Gary Faro/ Wayne Walker

BRIEF: To display colour transparencies in a light box manner that suggested stained glass windows; the displays are modular (Gothic, Norman, Islam) and mounted on casters

ATTENDANCE: Public

The interslotting components mounted round the central forum make a ridged shape to suggest buildings of different architectural styles. The overspill of illumination from the light box enhances the kiosks' tops.

are also t
would als
6-lane co
The Basi
London M
building,

London Docklands Development Corporation

PROJECT: Proposal for the development of the Royal Docks

DATE AND LOCATION: 1985, Royal Docks, London, England

PERMANENT, TRAVELLING OR ONE-OFF: Travelling; key elements were free standing and incorporated their own uplighters

SIZE (METRES OR FEET): Approximately 10 free-standing elements. The number of elements varied according to the available space. The first exhibition was approximately 150 sq m

DESIGNER: Williams and Phoa, London, England

BRIEF: To design an exhibition that reflected the character of the Royal Docks while communicating the necessary detailed information regarding their development. Part of the exhibition had to travel, some elements therefore had to be designed to work in isolation or as part of a larger set.

ATTENDANCE: Public, press, local government

IBM United Kingdom Ltd

PROJECT: Phase Four of IBM's North Harbour Headquarters

DATE AND LOCATION: 1983–1984; IBM Headquarters, London, England

PERMANENT, TRAVELLING OR ONE-OFF: One-off

SIZE (METRES OR FEET): Four double sided screens approx. 1.2 m x 2.2 m

DESIGNER: Arup Associates, London, England

BRIEF: To illustrate the new phase four of IBM's headquarters building

ATTENDANCE: IBM personnel

This system relies for its stability on a series of overhead crossbeams; the advantage is that the panels seem to levitate elegantly off the floor.

KaO Systems

PROJECT: New Arcade Gallery for Mansfield District Council

DATE AND LOCATION: May 1989, Mansfield, Nottinghamshire, England

PERMANENT, TRAVELLING OR ONE-OFF: Permanent

SIZE (METRES OR FEET): 90 sq m

DESIGNER: David Mackenzie and Zonya Bird/David Mackenzie Design, Lincoln, Lincolnshire, England

BRIEF: Arrangement of freestanding KaO units along one side of the gallery showing part of a social history display.

ATTENDANCE: Public

Trade Exhibitions

Every year, hundreds of exhibitions are held all over the world, each one intended to appeal to a specific customer. Spaces are booked months — even years — in advance if an exhibitor wants to get the best position. Sometimes the organizers will provide a shell scheme into which each company must fit its display; sometimes small imaginative solutions can be more impressive than giant double-decker constructions. Sometimes shows are held in hotel rooms or banqueting halls, where it is difficult to make an impact. And sometimes, elaborate buildings are refurbished or created especially for the event with moving auditoriums, catering facilities and the latest sound and lighting systems.

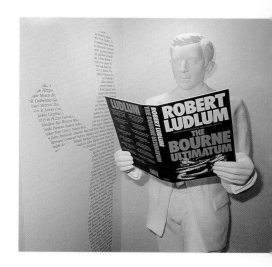

Union Carbide

PROJECT: Exhibit at Electrex

DATE AND LOCATION: 1984 , Electrex NEC,
Birmingham, England

PERMANENT, TRAVELLING OR ONE-OFF: One-off

SIZE (METRES OR FEET): 64 sq m

DESIGNER: Colin Thompson Design Associates,
London, England

BRIEF: To attract visitors to the launch of a new
range of products; a giant hand and electronic
components featured dramatically, and products
were also exhibited in life-sized hands.

ATTENDANCE: Trade

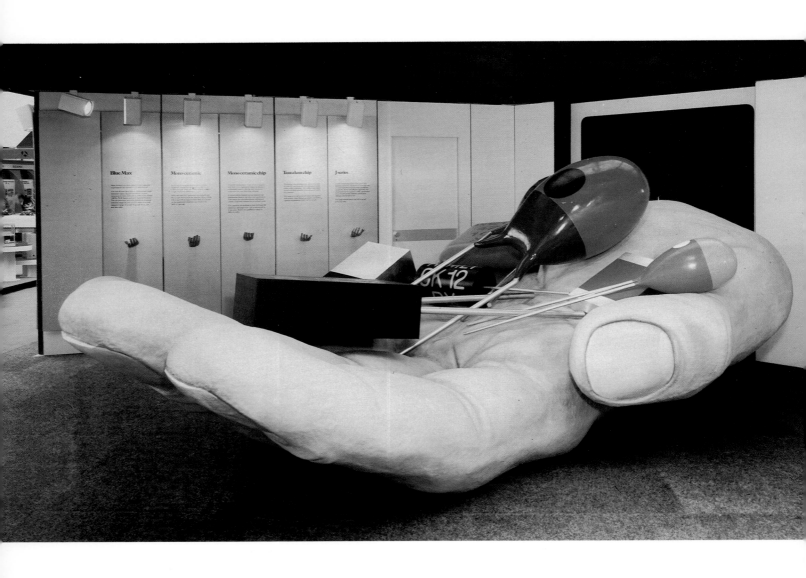

Dow Chemical Europe

PROJECT: Design Engineering Exhibition

DATE AND LOCATION: 1987, NEC, Birmingham, England

PERMANENT, TRAVELLING OR ONE-OFF: One-off

SIZE (METRES OR FEET): 48 sq m

DESIGNER: Colin Thompson Design Associates in conjunction with David Lock Design, London, England

BRIEF: To attract the attention of design engineers interested in new materials; development featured a four-metre enlargement of man's first footprint on the Moon.

ATTENDANCE: Trade

No product on display, but a clever use of mirrors gives twice as much impact to this lunar landscape.

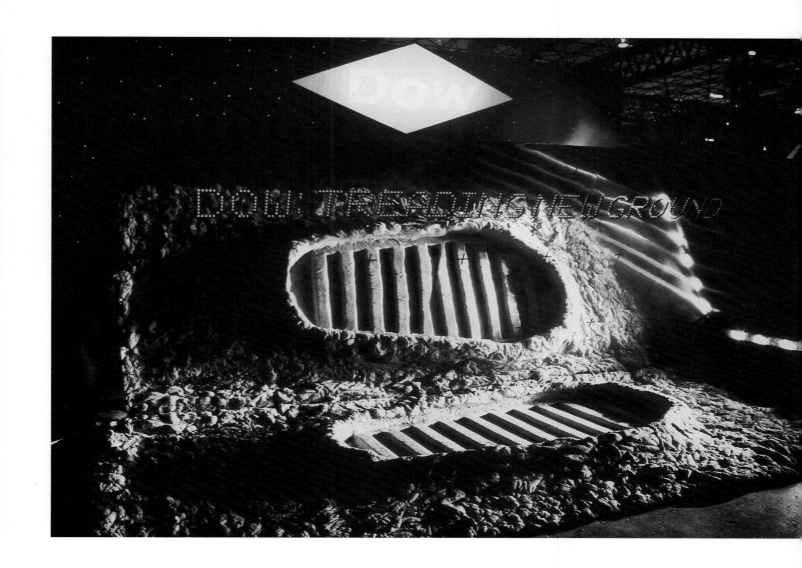

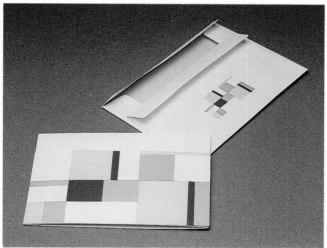

Mapasa

PROJECT: Exhibition stand and mailing

DATE AND LOCATION: March–April 1987, Construmat, Barcelona, Spain

PERMANENT, TRAVELLING OR ONE-OFF: One-off

SIZE (METRES OR FEET): 380 sq m

DESIGNER: Carmelo Hernando, Hernando Asociados, Barcelona, Spain

BRIEF: To design a stand to display the client's product, with room for corporate meetings; aimed at architects, construction industry and engineers.

ATTENDANCE: Trade

British Telecom

PROJECT: Stand at the 'Comm's '90' Exhibition

DATE AND LOCATION: April 1990, NEC, Birmingham, England

PERMANENT, TRAVELLING OR ONE-OFF: One-off

SIZE (METRES OR FEET): 793 sq m

DESIGNER: Imagination, London, England

BRIEF: To display latest developments in the client's technology and products.

ATTENDANCE: Trade

Despite the client's corporate colour being yellow at the time, this design team linked a series of semicircular building block structures with a circular 'runway' and a theme of pure white.

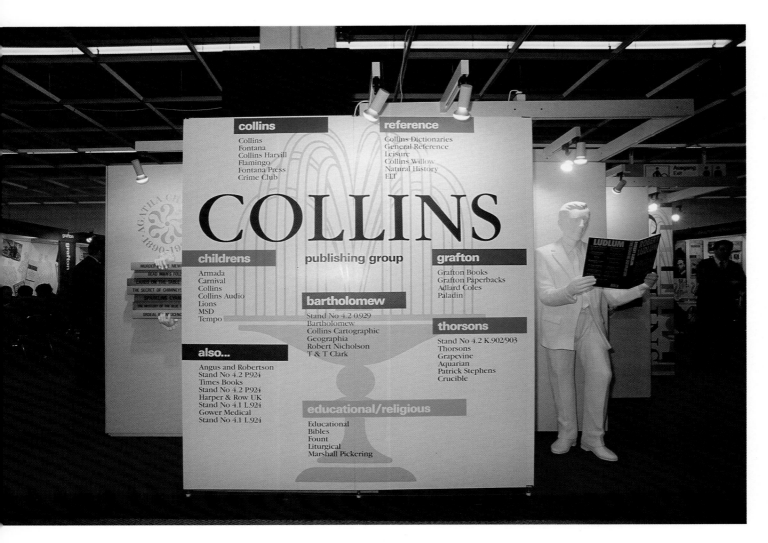

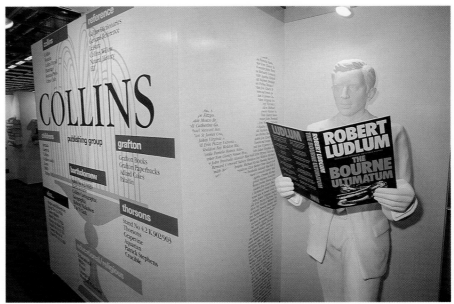

HarperCollins Publishers

PROJECT: Stand at Frankfurt Book Fair

DATE AND LOCATION: 1989, Frankfurt Book Fair, Germany

PERMANENT, TRAVELLING OR ONE-OFF: One-off

SIZE (METRES OR FEET): 187 sq m

DESIGNER: Terry Trickett, Jan Moscowitz, Alexandra Prescott/Trickett & Webb, London, England

BRIEF: To present a high profile image of the HarperCollins publishing conglomerate. The many separate publishing divisions of HarperCollins come together at Frankfurt, which explains why a family tree (or fountain) of companies formed a central feature of the exhibit. Visitors' attention was also gained by the surrealistic image of white hands puncturing the bland 'shell-scheme' walls; the invisible reader was apparently grasping the latest HarperCollins publications.

ATTENDANCE: Trade

Foreign and Commonwealth Office

PROJECT: Design Brittanico Exhibition

DATE AND LOCATION: 1990, Turin, Italy

PERMANENT, TRAVELLING OR ONE-OFF: Permanent

SIZE (METRES OR FEET): 570 sq m

DESIGNER: Nigel MacFall, Sarah Cadman/Minale
Tattersfield and Partners Ltd, London, England

BRIEF: To attract the interest of both industrialists
and the general public to establish mutually
beneficial trade links between Britain and Italy. The
stand had to display a variety of products.

ATTENDANCE: Public, trade

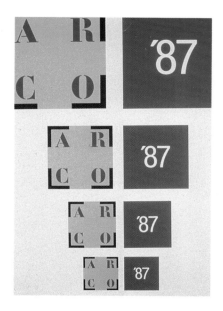

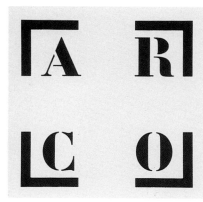

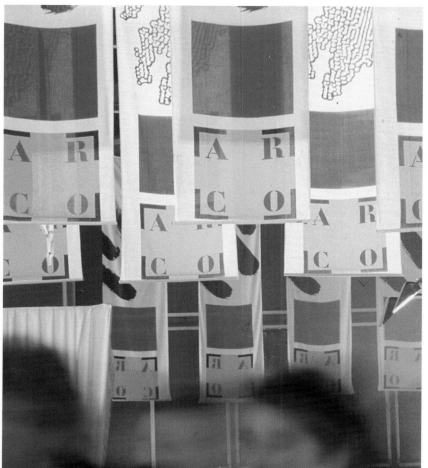

ARCO (International Exhibition of Contemporary Art)

PROJECT: Interior design for ARCO, the second most important exhibition of international contemporary art in the world.

DATE AND LOCATION: February 1987, IFEMA Crystal Palace, Madrid, Spain

PERMANENT, TRAVELLING OR ONE-OFF: One-off

SIZE (METRES OR FEET): 40,000 sq m

DESIGNER: Carlos Rolando/CR Communication and Design Services SA, Barcelona, Spain

BRIEF: To accommodate in one venue more than 200 art galleries from all countries to show the best of their artistic production. The fair is divided into several sections including drawing, sculpture, photography, graphic work, painting, video and multimedia; massive numbers of visitors also had to be taken into account.

ATTENDANCE: Public, trade

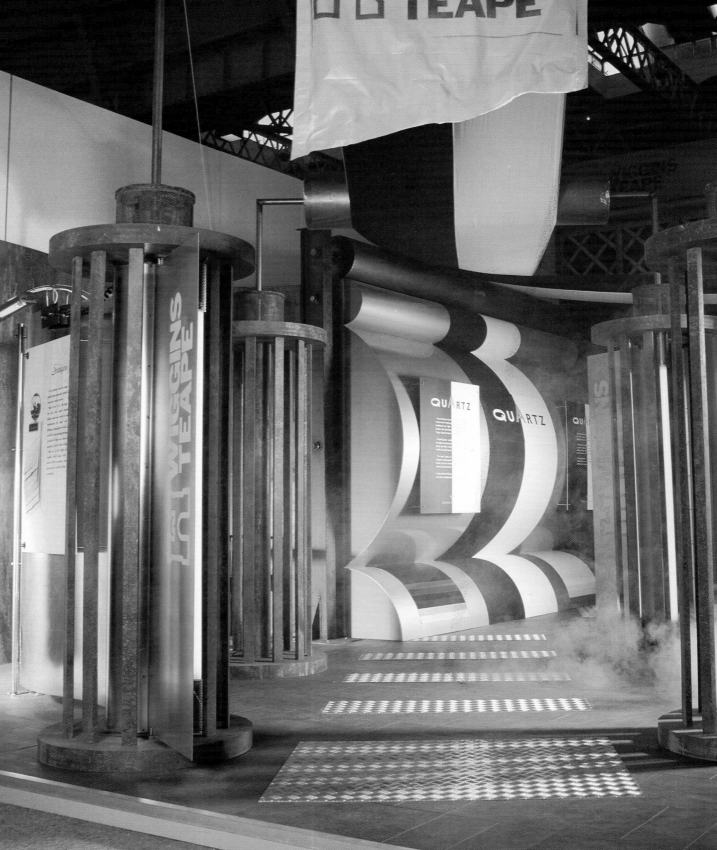

Wiggins Teape Fine Papers Ltd

PROJECT: National Graphics Exhibition

DATE AND LOCATION: 1988, National Graphic
Exhibition, Earl's Court, London, England

PPERMANENT, TRAVELLING OR ONE-OFF: One-off

SIZE (METRES OR FEET): 45 sq m

DESIGNER: Bowes Darby Design Associates,
London, England

BRIEF: To design and project-manage a
'showstopping' exhibition stand which would
portray Wiggins Teape as a design-conscious
organization at the forefront of its industry. The
focal point of the stand was the launch of a new
paper stock – 'quartz'. In design terms, the stand
needed to be exciting, innovative and unique.

ATTENDANCE: Trade

Coopers & Lybrand Network Services Group

PROJECT: Promotion for new service department

DATE AND LOCATION: October 1986, Telecommunication Managers Association Conference, Metropole, Brighton, East Sussex, England

PERMANENT, TRAVELLING OR ONE-OFF: One-off

SIZE (METRES OR FEET): 48 sq m

DESIGNER: The Association of Ideas Ltd, London, England

BRIEF: To communicate the problem solving abilities of Coopers & Lybrand and to provide on-stand meeting and interview space. No hardware on stand but six curvaceous panels filled with jargon are highlighted to say 'complex problems need straight talk'.

ATTENDANCE: Trade

Panels of endless, unillustrated text can never have looked more interesting – or more fun.

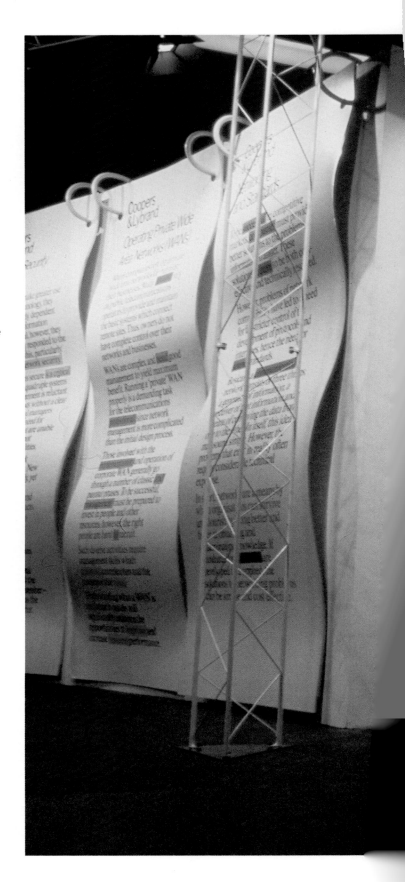

Hasbro Inc.

PROJECT: Buckley O'Hare (alien green rabbit, hero of comic book adventures)

DATE AND LOCATION: February 1991, Toy Fair, New York City, New York, USA

PERMANENT, TRAVELLING OR ONE-OFF: One-off within a permanent exhibit space for Hasbro Inc

SIZE (METRES OR FEET): 800 sq feet

DESIGNER: Don Campbell/Design Etc. Inc., New York City, New York, USA

BRIEF: To create a space in which the viewer could become a part of the comic book along with its protagonists

ATTENDANCE: Trade, public

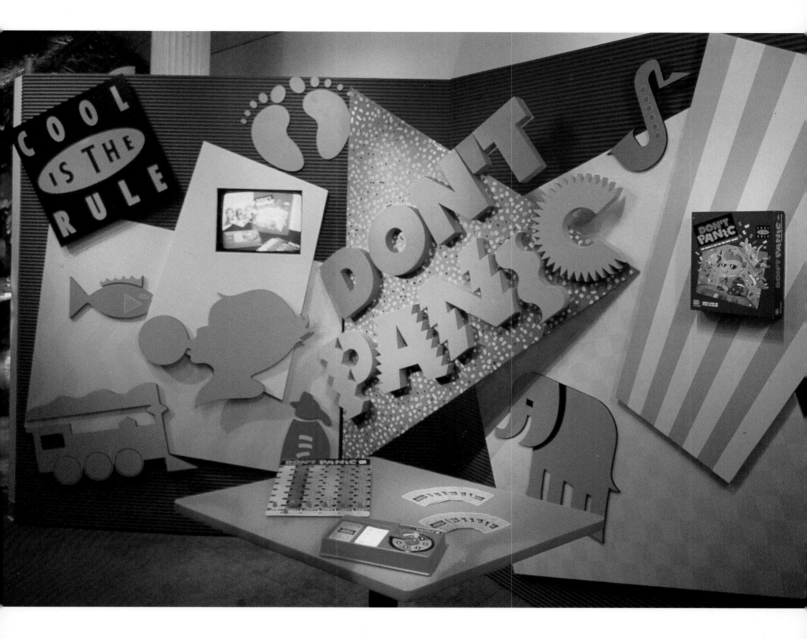

Milton Bradley Games

PROJECT: Don't Panic – the name-a-lot-on-the-spot
game

DATE AND LOCATION: February 1991, Toy Fair, New
York City, New York, USA

PERMANENT, TRAVELLING OR ONE-OFF: One-off

SIZE (METRES OR FEET): 190 sq feet

DESIGNER: Randy Benjamin/Design Etc. Inc., New
York City, New York, USA

BRIEF: To encapsulate the spirit and image of Milton
Bradley Games. The visitor is immersed in a graphic
environment intended to make the world of games
come alive.

ATTENDANCE: Trade, public

Milton Bradley Games

PROJECT: Exhibits at Salon du Jouet, Paris, France

DATE AND LOCATION: 1986, Salon du Jouet, Paris, France

PERMANENT, TRAVELLING OR ONE-OFF: One-off

SIZE (METRES OR FEET): 750 sq m each

DESIGNER: ADSA & Partners, Paris, France

BRIEF: To provide exhibits to excite the visitors curiosity and entice them into a 'magic world'. Each exhibit was subdivided into small spaces, each one a tiny world inhabited by the product on display.

ATTENDANCE: Trade

Oracle UK

PROJECT: Computers in Manufacturing

DATE AND LOCATION: October 1990, NEC
Birmingham, England

PERMANENT, TRAVELLING OR ONE-OFF: One-off

SIZE (METRES OR FEET): 210 sq m

DESIGNER: GLS Design, London, England

BRIEF: To design high quality components to
establish and maintain the 'Oracle Image' in
various display situations. The formula of backlit
logos, workstations, graphic panels, lighting and
traditional build can be used for all levels and sizes
of stands.

ATTENDANCE: Public

John Heyer for Zanders Paper Manufacturers

PROJECT: Production of company reports and accounts on Zanders paper

DATE AND LOCATION: January 1989, The Old Whitbread Brewery, London, England

PERMANENT, TRAVELLING OR ONE-OFF: One-off

SIZE (METRES OR FEET): 1900 sq feet

DESIGNER: DCS Fairs Limited, London, England

BRIEF: To provide an attractive and functional area designed to represent a paper manufacturer and to show off their products.

ATTENDANCE: Trade

The most dramatic and innovative aspect of this exhibit is the use of the floor.

Wang

PROJECT: 'Wang delivers the Office' stand

DATE AND LOCATION: February 1986, Which
Computer Show, NEC, Birmingham, England

PPERMANENT, TRAVELLING OR ONE-OFF: One-off

SIZE (METRES OR FEET): 112 sq m

DESIGNER: David Hall/Firbank Kempster Group,
London, England

BRIEF: To produce a highly original, attention-
grabbing exhibit to promote the product; the
theme was built round the title, by putting a
package of products into individual packing like
displays.

ATTENDANCE: Trade

Scale is an element that exhibition designers can
often use to great effect.

Peer-Logic

PROJECT: Trade stand to advertise new corporate identity

DATE AND LOCATION: 1990, Networld, Dallas, Texas, USA

PERMANENT, TRAVELLING OR ONE-OFF: Travelling

SIZE (METRES OR FEET): 400 sq m

DESIGNER: Lynn Neff, Conover Smith/Color & Design Exhibits Inc, San Jose, California, USA

BRIEF: To provide a stand that would reflect the corporate re-profiling and name change undertaken by the client as they broke away from a larger company. An 'under construction' theme was used to maximise exposure .

ATTENDANCE: Trade

Shipping crates (painted and stencilled) form the backwall, draped with oversized painters' canvas. This inexpensive solution allowed the client more of the budget to spend on exhibit components; the client wanted to use as much of the exhibit as possible on subsequent fairs and shows.

BBC Enterprises

PROJECT: BBC Showcase

DATE AND LOCATION: 1988, Brighton Centre, Brighton, East Sussex, England

PERMANENT, TRAVELLING OR ONE-OFF: One-off

SIZE (METRES OR FEET): 2000 sq m

DESIGNER: Mark Thompson and John Shaw/ Elevations, Denton, Northamptonshire, England

BRIEF: To turn the Brighton Centre into a comfortable yet businesslike environment where international TV buyers could meet, view and select programmes.

ATTENDANCE: Trade

Complicated planning requirements and space allocations have been overcome by the use of perforated fins and unifying kite-shaped sails off which light is bounced.

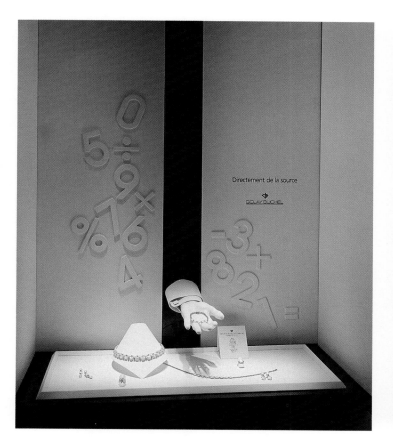

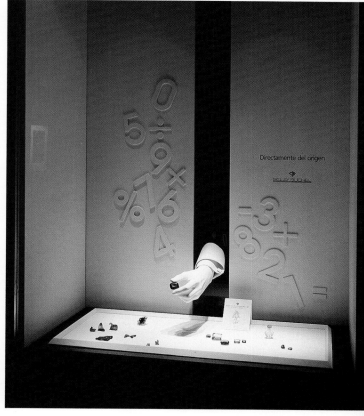

Golay Buchel et Cie

PROJECT: Window displays of jewellery and
precious stones

DATE AND LOCATION: 1990 European Watch and
Jewellery Fair, Basle, Switzerland

PERMANENT, TRAVELLING OR ONE-OFF: One-off

SIZE (METRES OR FEET): 8 sq m

DESIGNER: Maurice Progin ASG, Lausanne,
Switzerland

BRIEF: To produce an exhibition stand showing 'The
Best Offer' of the client in a shop window format.

ATTENDANCE: Trade

Aferfrans SA

PROJECT: Stand at Alimentaria Trade Fair

DATE AND LOCATION: 1990, Barcelona, Spain

PERMANENT, TRAVELLING OR ONE-OFF: One-off

SIZE (METRES OR FEET): 180 sq m

DESIGNER: Esteve Agulló and Mariano Pi/Quod, Barcelona, Spain

BRIEF: To display the products of wine and spirits distributors Aferfrans, focusing on luxury ranges such as Chandon cava and Möet et Chandon champagne.

ATTENDANCE: Trade

The overscaled canvas fascia to this stand places the client's brands where everyone can see them without any sense of brashness or clutter. The 'washed' lighting throughout the interior gives an added feeling of calm and luxury.

Warerite

PROJECT: Exhibit at Interior Design International
DATE AND LOCATION: 1989, Interior Design
International, Earl's Court, London, England
PERMANENT, TRAVELLING OR ONE-OFF: One-off
SIZE (METRES OR FEET): 600 sq feet
DESIGNER: Rasshied Din, Kirsty Moon/Din
Associates, London, England
BRIEF: To design a stand to attract designer/
specifiers to a good quality product whose image
was considered by its manufacturers to be slightly
boring in comparison to the competition.
ATTENDANCE: Trade

Warerite 1989 continued over page

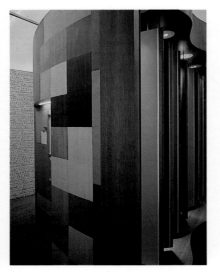

Warerite

PROJECT: Exhibit at Interior Design International

DATE AND LOCATION: 1990, Interior Design International, Earl's Court, London, England

PERMANENT, TRAVELLING OR ONE-OFF: One-off

SIZE (METRES OR FEET): 500 sq feet

DESIGNER: John Harvey, Kirsty Moon/Din Associates, London, England

BRIEF: To produce a second design (after the success of 1989's version) presenting a new range of natural finish laminates; an illustration was also used, enlarged and laminated to produce a screen.

ATTENDANCE: Trade, public

Warerite

PROJECT: Exhibit at Public Services Exhibition

DATE AND LOCATION: April 1990, Bushey Design Centre, Hertfordshire, England

PERMANENT, TRAVELLING OR ONE-OFF: One-off

SIZE (METRES OR FEET): 250 sq feet

DESIGNER: Valerie Wickes, Kate Good/Din Associates, London, England

BRIEF: To show how versatile laminate can be; this was a simple graphic exercise to produce, but a complicated manufacturing process. The exhibit showed how specifiers could customize laminate.

ATTENDANCE: Trade

Pepe Jeans

PROJECT: Mens' Retail Trade Show

DATE AND LOCATION: 1989, Olympia, London, England

PERMANENT, TRAVELLING OR ONE-OFF: Travelling

SIZE (METRES OR FEET): 400 – 650 sq feet

DESIGNER: Rasshied Din, Angela Drinkall/Din Associates, London, England

BRIEF: To design a stand based on Florence railway station to present a working theme to the product.

ATTENDANCE: Trade

A good example of the incredible range of inspiration sources available to designers and enlightened clients.

London Brick Company

PROJECT: Display at Interbuild Exhibition

DATE AND LOCATION: 1989, NEC Birmingham, England

PERMANENT, TRAVELLING OR ONE-OFF: One-off

SIZE (METRES OR FEET): 336 sq m

DESIGNER: Trickett and Webb, London, England

BRIEF: To 'do the impossible with brick'.
Experience has shown that architects and specifiers are much more likely to step on the stand if their sense of wonder and disbelief is first roused. Within the brick sculpture garden (London Brick's 1989 theme), the exhibit which attracted most attention was 'OXO', an interlinked series of brick rings, huge in scale, whose apparent lack of support gave an illusion of weightlessness.

ATTENDANCE: Trade

House of Shutters

PROJECT: Wooden window shutters exhibit

DATE AND LOCATION: Spring 1990, Interior Design International, Earl's Court, London, England

PERMANENT, TRAVELLING OR ONE-OFF: One-off (but used twice at short four day exhibitions)

SIZE (METRES OR FEET): 40 sq m

DESIGNER: Sarah Charles, London, England

BRIEF: To create a stand that had the quality of a light box – a jewel of brightness that would immediately attract the visitor's eye.

ATTENDANCE: Trade

Forrec Design Europe

PROJECT: Leisure Industry Week

DATE AND LOCATION: October 1990, NEC, Birmingham, England

PERMANENT, TRAVELLING OR ONE-OFF: One-off

SIZE (METRES OR FEET): 250 sq feet

DESIGNER: Foley Cooke Design Consultants, London, England

BRIEF: To provide a simple high-tech backdrop for the display of completed projects in photographic and illustrative form.

ATTENDANCE: Trade

A strong and satisfying combination of black uprights and horizontal graphic panels; every detail seems carefully considered and neatly integrated, including the client's logo embossed in white.

AGB Publications Ltd

PROJECT: *Interior Design Magazine* Awards

DATE AND LOCATION: May 1989, Interior Design
International, Earl's Court, London, England

PERMANENT, TRAVELLING OR ONE-OFF: One-off

SIZE (METRES OR FEET): 1500 sq feet

DESIGNER: Foley Cooke Design Consultants,
London, England

BRIEF: To exhibit the *Interior Design Magazine*
Awards for 1989 and provide a subscription area.

ATTENDANCE: Trade

Zanotta

PROJECT: Stand at the Milan Furniture Fair

DATE AND LOCATION: April 1991, Salon del Mobile, Milan, Italy

PERMANENT, TRAVELLING OR ONE-OFF: One-off

SIZE (METRES OR FEET): 486 sq m

DESIGNER: Achille Castiglioni Architect, Milan, Italy; graphics: Italo Lupi

BRIEF: To make a dramatic display of the client's products.

ATTENDANCE: Trade

Musée des Arts Décoratifs

PROJECT: Techniques Discrètes: Furniture Design in Italy 1980–1990

DATE AND LOCATION: April 1991, Musée des Arts Décoratifs, Paris, France

PERMANENT, TRAVELLING OR ONE-OFF: One-off

SIZE (METRES OR FEET): 1200 sq m

DESIGNER: Achille Castiglioni and Michele De Lucchi, Milan, Italy

BRIEF: To design an exhibition to show off the best in contemporary Italian furniture design.

ATTENDANCE: Public

Cassina

PROJECT: Exhibition at furniture showroom

DATE AND LOCATION: April 1991, Milan, Italy

PERMANENT, TRAVELLING OR ONE-OFF: One-off

SIZE (METRES OR FEET): 1125 sq m

DESIGNER: Achille Castiglioni Architect, Milan, Italy; graphics: Italo Lupi

BRIEF: To display Cassina furniture and focus attention on the leather used in the client's product.

ATTENDANCE: Trade, public

173

Ingo Maurer GmbH

PROJECT: Exhibition of lighting and 'clocks' produced in cooperation with Ron Arad, London, England

DATE AND LOCATION: April 1991, La Fabbrica del Vappore, Milan, Italy

PERMANENT, TRAVELLING OR ONE-OFF: One-off

SIZE (METRES OR FEET): 800 sq m

DESIGNER: Ingo Maurer GmbH, Munich, Germany

BRIEF: To make a dramatic display of lighting to show how it may be used in various retail and display conditions.

ATTENDANCE: Trade, public

Held in a deserted warehouse during the Milan Furniture Fair, this bold piece of theatre juxtaposes high quality finishes and modern technology with the crumbling texture of the old building.

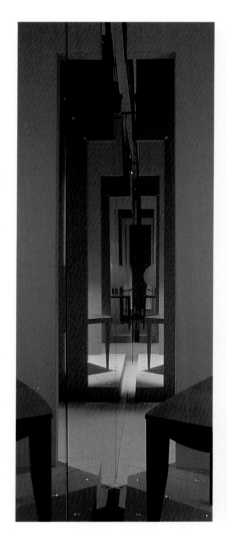

Sawaya & Moroni

PROJECT: Sawaya & Moroni Stand, Milan Furniture Fair

DATE AND LOCATION: April 1991, Salone del Mobile, Milan, Italy

PPERMANENT, TRAVELLING OR ONE-OFF: One-off

SIZE (METRES OR FEET): 78 sq m

DESIGNER: William K. Sawaya, Sawaya & Moroni, Milan, Italy

BRIEF: To promote Sawaya & Moroni products: the stand area was at the end of a long, narrow corridor; interest and curiosity was stimulated by giant columns. Light and colour were used with a mirrored wall to give the impression of a vast space.

ATTENDANCE: Trade, public

A wonderful sense of space and volume is created by the almost sensual use of hollow columns, each one sliced to let the glowing colour within spill out. Individual products are displayed within each structure.

Ideal Standard

PROJECT: Interbuild Exhibition

DATE AND LOCATION: November/December 1989, NEC, Birmingham, England

PERMANENT, TRAVELLING OR ONE-OFF: One-off

SIZE (METRES OR FEET): 1800 sq ft

DESIGNER: Peter Leonard Associates, London, England

BRIEF: To promote Ideal Standard as Europe's leading bathroom equipment manufacturers.

ATTENDANCE: Trade, public

'Raising the roof' on this basically straightforward structure gives animation, adds lightness and draws attention. Water runs down the face of the graphics panel as it once did in the windows of fish shops.

Pierre Frey

PROJECT: Exhibition stand at Furniture Fair held
every two years

DATE AND LOCATION: January 1991, Grand Palais,
Paris, France

PERMANENT, TRAVELLING OR ONE-OFF: One-off

SIZE (METRES OR FEET): 300 sq m .

DESIGNER: Jaques Luzeau, Alix de Dives, Pierre Frey,
Paris, France

BRIEF: To present the new collection of Pierre Frey
designs (fabrics, wallcoverings and wallpapers)

ATTENDANCE: Trade

Salon Moving International

PROJECT: Le Grand Magasin

DATE AND LOCATION: September 1990, Salon
Moving International, Paris, France

PERMANENT, TRAVELLING OR ONE-OFF: One-off

SIZE (METRES OR FEET): 400 sq m on two levels

DESIGNER: Henri Mendonça Architect; Stylist:
Michéle Chauvel

BRIEF: To display the latest innovatory products
based on the theme of 'Le Grand Magasin'.

ATTENDANCE: Trade

Scènes D'Intérieur

PROJECT: *Les Tendances de la Décoration: Hémisphère Sud*

DATE AND LOCATION: September 1989, Salon International de la Décoration, Levallois, France

PERMANENT, TRAVELLING OR ONE-OFF: One-off

SIZE (METRES OR FEET): 100–120 sq m

DESIGNER: Nelly Rodi/Scènes d'Intérieur, Paris, France

BRIEF: To show latest trends in interior decoration displayed in house settings

ATTENDANCE: Trade

Each year buyers of household products from all over the world head for Paris to see all the latest merchandise: floorcoverings, gifts, fabrics and wallpapers, lighting, bedlinen and tableware are all shown in a series of trade fairs including Moving, Scènes d'Intérieur, Parallele Bijorhca and the famous Biennale des Editeurs de la Decoration. Each fair contains a display of what it sees as the latest trends or 'tendances'.

Agence +4D

PROJECT: Exhibit at Salon Moving International

DATE AND LOCATION: September 1990

PERMANENT, TRAVELLING OR ONE-OFF: One-off

SIZE (METRES OR FEET): 18 sq m

DESIGNER: François Ligori/Padco Blenheim/Groupe
Blenheim, Levallois, France

BRIEF: To display client's furniture range.

ATTENDANCE: Trade

Modern furniture, displayed in a setting more like a
window display than any traditional concept of
exhibition design. This stand was voted the best in
the exhibition by the professional press.

Daum

PROJECT: Exhibit for Scènes d'Intérieur

DATE AND LOCATION: September 1989, Salon
International de la Décoration, Levallois, France

PERMANENT, TRAVELLING OR ONE-OFF: One-off

SIZE (METRES OR FEET): 54 sq m

DESIGNER: Clothilde Bacri and Hilton McConnico
Salon Scènes d'Intérieur, Paris, France

BRIEF: To display glass products

ATTENDANCE: Trade

Each year the famous French glass manufacturer
displays its latest products in a setting designed by
some of Paris's top stylists.

Lilicolor

PROJECT: Stand to exhibit new range of fabrics, carpets and wall-coverings

DATE AND LOCATION: January 1991, Japan Convention Centre (Makahuri Messe) Tokyo, Japan

PERMANENT, TRAVELLING OR ONE-OFF: One-off

SIZE (METRES OR FEET): 350 sq m

DESIGNER: Kouichi Takaku/Tachmic; Haruyasu Arita/Kobayashi Kogei-sha Co Ltd, Tokyo, Japan

BRIEF: To bring the new range of products to the attention of the trade customers and designers; a dynamic blend of design and colour seeks to express a Caribbean rhythm.

ATTENDANCE: Public

The Japanese idea of the Caribbean isn't the same as mine, but the design team certainly had fun.

Ohbayashi Corporation and NEC Corporation

PROJECT: Super high-rise buildings; Ohbayashi erected a six-metre booth and projector; NEC showed building maintenance system products.

DATE AND LOCATION: February 1991, My Dome, Osaka, Japan

PERMANENT, TRAVELLING OR ONE-OFF: One-off

SIZE (METRES OR FEET): 162 sq m

DESIGNER: Mitsuhiro Hirose/Nomura Co Ltd, Tokyo, Japan

BRIEF: To promote the lifestyle in the Kansai area of Japan. The economy is different from Tokyo, with intelligent buildings playing a special role in the office environment. Using reflecting and transparent surfaces, a world of mirrors is represented. Even the floor of the booth is reflective.

ATTENDANCE: Trade

The Kenwood Corporation

PROJECT: New radio equipment with emphasis on car and hand systems

DATE AND LOCATION: August 1990, Tokyo International Trade Centre, Tokyo, Japan

PERMANENT, TRAVELLING OR ONE-OFF: One-off

SIZE (METRES OR FEET): 16.2 × 7.2 m

DESIGNER: Susumu Maehara, Tetsuo Uba, Haruyasu Arita/Kobayashi Kogei-Sha Co Ltd, Tokyo, Japan

BRIEF: To emphasize an active lifestyle in a natural outdoor scene (the keyword is Kenwood Forest); the aim was to promote radio use among the general public as well as amateurs and radio buffs.

ATTENDANCE: Public

Matsushita Electric Industrial Co Ltd

PROJECT: A Matsushita Electric Show at Audio Fair

DATE AND LOCATION: October 1989, Ikebukuro Sunshine Building, Tokyo, Japan

PERMANENT, TRAVELLING OR ONE-OFF: One-off

SIZE (METRES OR FEET): 384 sq m

DESIGNER: Takahiro Kurihara, Hiroshi Imanaka/ Nomura Co Ltd, Tokyo, Japan

BRIEF: To exhibit the newest technology in a 'Time Machine' that slips back to ancient days, vividly showing the great difference between past and present.

ATTENDANCE: Public

One way to attract attention – and liven up a rather austere exhibit. Exhibitions, although photographed when empty, will always be experienced crowded with thousands of visitors.

Sharp Corporation

PROJECT: An audio-visual exhibit centering on liquid crystal display technology

DATE AND LOCATION: October 1990 Harumi International Trade Centre, Tokyo, Japan

PERMANENT, TRAVELLING OR ONE-OFF: One-off

SIZE (METRES OR FEET): 315 sq m

DESIGNER: Akio Koide, Takao Onishi, Shin'ya Shiga/Nomura Co Ltd, Tokyo, Japan

BRIEF: To provide unusual interior display to accent the appeal of LCD innovations.

ATTENDANCE: Public

Thousands of tiny TV screens replace the usual display panels and overwhelm with their simple symmetry.

NEC Corporation

PROJECT: Computer products trade show
DATE AND LOCATION: May 1990, Harumi
International Trade Centre, Tokyo, Japan
PERMANENT, TRAVELLING OR ONE-OFF: One-off
SIZE (METRES OR FEET): 1000 sq m and 550 sq m
DESIGNER: Yuji Hirata/Nomura Co Ltd, Tokyo, Japan
BRIEF: To promote computers and other products in
the computer field. Horizontal lighting was used to
bathe the computers in a soft ambience.
ATTENDANCE: Trade

Interestingly, the text panels seem almost an
afterthought compared to careful integration or all
the other elements into the overall structure.

Philips Electrics

PROJECT: Philips Trade Fair Exhibition stand

DATE AND LOCATION: November 1987, NEC,
Birmingham, England

PERMANENT, TRAVELLING OR ONE-OFF: One-off

SIZE (METRES OR FEET): 170 sq m

DESIGNER: Firbank Kempster Group, London, England

BRIEF: To produce an attractive, attention-getting
stand which maximises the strength of the Philips
logo. The client wanted to make inroads into the
designer custom-built kitchen market and increase
market share; also to launch new products.

ATTENDANCE: Trade

Epson

PROJECT: Computer exhibit

DATE AND LOCATION: February 1989, Which
Computer Show, NEC, Birmingham, England

PERMANENT, TRAVELLING OR ONE-OFF: One-off

SIZE (METRES OR FEET): 430 sq m

DESIGNER: Dave Hobday Design, London, England;
construction: Estdale Exhibitions; sculptor: Derek
Howorth

BRIEF: To display a full range of computers and
printers in a novel way to attract the widest
audience. The theme – the word is "mightier than
the sword" used on all computer and printer
demonstrations based on a wide variety of literary
quotations. The centre-piece was a three-metre
high computer made from books with a sword
broken across it.

ATTENDANCE: Trade, public

Difficult to have fun with this type of product, but
this stand effectively succeeds without
undermining the product's integrity or insulting its
audience.

3M UK plc Automotive Trade Division

PROJECT: Exhibit for Motor Show

DATE AND LOCATION: November 1989, NEC,
Birmingham, England

PERMANENT, TRAVELLING OR ONE-OFF: One-off

SIZE (METRES OR FEET): 110 sq m

DESIGNER: Dave Hobday Design, London, England;
contractor: Hicken Exhibitions

BRIEF: To display several hundred diverse products
used in motor vehicle production ranging from
adhesives and abrasives to electronic components.
The display wall was presented as a 'chequered
flag', the modules both containing and integrating
the varied product range and of course implying
the image of "The winner". The rainbow and cloud
was a lighting feature to attract attention and raise
spirits.

Lotus Development UK Ltd

PROJECT: Computer Software Exhibit

DATE AND LOCATION: November 1990 and January 1991, OS/2 Show and IC Conference, Olympia 2, London, England

PERMANENT, TRAVELLING OR ONE-OFF: One-offs

SIZE (METRES OR FEET): 50 sq m and 60 sq m

DESIGNER: Davie Hobday Design, London, England; contractor: Estdale Exhibitons; scenic artist: George Thain

BRIEF: To exhibit and demonstrate three software products. The design centred on a scenic wall painting based on the drawings of the 17th century theologian Robert Fludd. Fludd's attempts to express abstract ideas graphically was exactly what today's software developers are attempting.

ATTENDANCE: Computer trade, public

Hewlett-Packard

PROJECT : Triple-deck exhibition stand

DATE AND LOCATION : 1987, Geneva, Switzerland

PERMANENT, TRAVELLING OR ONE-OFF : One-off

SIZE (METRES OR FEET) : 324 sq m

DESIGNER : Furneaux Stewart Design Limited,
London, England

BRIEF : To design a stand that would make a lasting
impression of Hewlett-Packard upon its visitors and
that would reinforce the perception of the
company's products as one of 'total capability'.

ATTENDANCE : Trade

Although the space available was relatively small, a
high impact architectural feature was created by
persuading the organizers to allow a 100%
increase in build height. The resulting triple-deck
structure effectively doubled the available floor
space and incorporated product displays, 40-seater
audience lift, a presentation theatre and VIP deck.
The striking effect here is created not by the
graphics or the choice of materials but by the bold,
uncluttered wedge-shape.

Citroen UK Ltd

PROJECT: Exhibition stand at Motor Show

DATE AND LOCATION: 1991, Fleet Show '91, Olympia, London, England

PERMANENT, TRAVELLING OR ONE-OFF: One-off

SIZE (METRES OR FEET): 589 sq m

DESIGNER: Furneaux Stewart Design Limited, London, England

BRIEF: To design an exhibition stand that would make Citroen's range of vehicles stand out in the show that influences the fleet-buying decisions of Britain's major companies; also to incorporate suitable hospitality facilities for a targetted, pre-invited audience.

ATTENDANCE: Trade

The design solution centres on a visually exciting stretched fabric structure. Designed to form a dramatic shape, this structure provides the stand with a clear focus and draws the eye irresistibly towards it and the cars being displayed. The design incorporated a central, double-decked structure housing the hospitality area on the upper deck.

Citroen continued over page

Fusion

PROJECT: 'Driving Ambition' hospitality complex

DATE AND LOCATION: 199, Millbrook, Bedfordshire, England

PERMANENT, TRAVELLING OR ONE-OFF: Permanent

SIZE (METRES OR FEET): Curved wall feature measures 120m × 13.5m at its highest point

DESIGNER: Furneaux Stewart Design Limited, London, England

BRIEF: To design a permanent hospitality complex on the site of the Millbrook Vehicle Proving Ground to accommodate Fusion's 'Driving Ambition' corporate hospitality event which uses the driving circuits of the Proving Ground. The internal spaces of the complex were required to be flexible and capable of accommodating clients' exhibitions, product launches and conferences as well as incorporating a restaurant and providing branding opportunities to enable clients to 'own' the facility during their events.

ATTENDANCE: Public and trade depending on the event

The silver geodesic domes convert to audio-visual theatres and restaurants as required, accommodating up to 120 people in each one and the curved wall structure can house larger-scale product launches and conferences as well as providing superb branding opportunities externally.

Porsche Cars Great Britain Limited

PROJECT: Exhibit at Motor Show

DATE AND LOCATION: 1988, International Motor Show, NEC, Birmingham England

PERMANENT, TRAVELLING OR ONE-OFF: One-off

SIZE (METRES OR FEET): 21.5m × 33m

DESIGNER: Furneaux Stewart Design Limited, London, England

BRIEF: To design a public exhibition which would display the cars in the most exciting manner possible to maintain a high profile for Porsche; one of the requirements was for an internal private hospitality suite for pre-invited potential customers.

ATTENDANCE: Trade

The stand was also required to be re-usable – the revolving discs, for example, were designed to be operated individually for smaller promotions afterwards. The theme could also be used for subsequent promotions: 'Kinetic Art' became the theme of the exhibition and was reflected both in the fluid movement of the cars on the discs and the stand graphics.

Ford Motors

PROJECT: Public launch of the Orion range

DATE AND LOCATION: September 1990,
International Motor Show, NEC, Birmingham,
England

PERMANENT, TRAVELLING OR ONE-OFF: One-off

SIZE (METRES OR FEET): 4000 sq m

DESIGNER: Imagination, London, England

BRIEF: To design an exciting launch concept for the
client's new product.

ATTENDANCE: Trade and public

Nobody in the UK knows more about the theatre of
launching cars than Imagination.

BMW AG

PROJECT: Stand at International Motor Show

DATE AND LOCATION: October 1988, NEC Birmingham, England

PERMANENT, TRAVELLING OR ONE-OFF: One-off

SIZE (METRES OR FEET): 912 sq m

DESIGNER: Rüdi Müller, Chris Harbecke, Leo Walser. Zintzmeyer & Lux AG, Zurich, Switzerland Switzerland

BRIEF: To introduce 5 Series into UK in a featured presentation; The main attraction was a six-metre high unit on one end of the building, visible from both upper and lower levels. Lights pointed onto the car and multimedia show behind were synchronized and controlled by a computer, allowing images such as the interior, engines or transmission to be projected onto the real car.

ATTENDANCE: Trade, public

BMW AG

PROJECT: Stand at the 59th International Motor
Show

DATE AND LOCATION: March 1989, Salon
Internationale de l'Automobile, Geneva,
Switzerland

PERMANENT, TRAVELLING OR ONE-OFF: One-off

SIZE (METRES OR FEET): 13,000 sq m

DESIGNER: Rüdi Müller and Leo Walser/Zintzmeyer &
Lux AG, Zurich, Switzerland

BRIEF: To show the full BMW range and distinguish
between the 3, 5 and 7 Series. To reflect the
heirarchy of the cars, the entire ground floor was
laid out in granite. For the 3 Series, the outer floor
area is rough textured granite; one step up, the 5
Series cars are displayed on sanded granite; on the
third level, the exclusive 7 Series sits on polished
granite. Behind a titled 'S' shaped glass wall is the
VIP zone, displaying the most expensive cars in a
quiet, reverential environment reminiscent of a
bank lobby.

ATTENDANCE: Trade, public

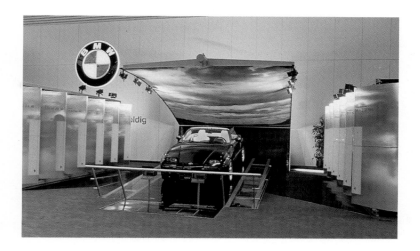

BMW AG

PROJECT: Stand at Amsterdam Auto Show

DATE AND LOCATION: February 1989, RAI, Amsterdam, Netherlands

PERMANENT, TRAVELLING OR ONE-OFF: One-off

SIZE (METRES OR FEET): 1350 sq m

DESIGNER: Rüdi Müller, Benjamin Thut, Leo Walser/ Zintzmeyer & Lux AG, Zurich, Switzerland

BRIEF: To show off the full range of BMW products and to project a strong brand image; different environments were provided for each car line. At the rear of the stand is a double deck multimedia of glass tilted at 45 degrees.

ATTENDANCE: Trade, public

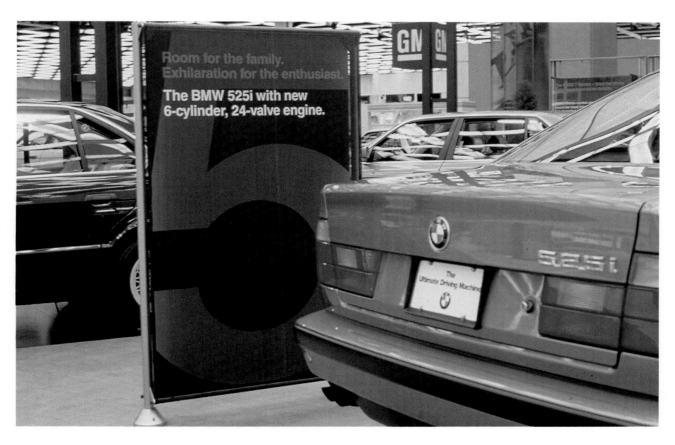

BMW AG

PROJECT: Stand at the North American Auto Show
DATE AND LOCATION: January 1991, North American
International Auto Show, Detroit, Michigan, USA
PERMANENT, TRAVELLING OR ONE-OFF: One-off
SIZE (METRES OR FEET): 12 100 sq ft
DESIGNER: Rüdi Müller, Peter Dixon, Masahiro
Ogyu, Benjamin Thut/Zintzmeyer & Lux AG, Zurich,
Switzerland
BRIEF: To illustrate the design philosophy
underlaying the BMW product; the philosophy of
showing rather than hiding, of functional
integrity tempered by refinement and aesthetic
consideration; materials and their finishes express
themselves; communication elements are
engineered and express their construction.
This approach, when combined with the
meticulous attention to detail underlines the
straightforward quality of the product.
ATTENDANCE: Trade, public

Index of Projects

W

Z

Directory of Practising Designers

This directory lists the addresses of designers in current practice. While every effort has been made to ensure that this list was correct at the time of going to press, subsequent changes in address or status are beyond the publishers' remit.

ADSA & Partners
74 rue du Faubourg St Antoine, 75012 Paris, France
PROJECT: Milton Bradley Games 140–1

Arup Associates
2 Dean Street, London W1V 6QB, England
PROJECT: IBM United Kingdom Ltd 116

The Association of Ideas
9 Paddington Street, London W1M 3LA, England
PROJECTS: Cooper & Lybrand 136–7; Friends of the Earth 114–5

Bowes Darby
Magdalen House, 136 Tooley Street, London SE1 2TU, England
PROJECT: Wiggins Teape 134–5

Bremner & Orr Design
Alderley House, 53 Long Street, Tetbury, Gloucestershire GL8 8AA, England
PROJECT: Devizes Museum, Wiltshire 76–7

The Burdick Group
35 South Park, San Francisco, California 94107–1877, USA
PROJECTS: Dow Plastics 96–7; San Francisco Primate Center 62–3

CR Communications & Design Services
Reina Victoria 24, 08021 Barcelona, Spain
PROJECTS: ARCO 132–3; La Carpa de la Ciencia 88–9

Carter Wong
29 Brook Mews North, London W2 3BW, England
PROJECTS: Design Museum 112–3; Shell International 94–5

Dr Architetto Achille Castiglioni
Piazza Castello 27, 20121 Milan, Italy
PROJECTS: Cassina 172–3; Techniques Discrètes 170–1; Zanotta 168–9

Central Exhibitions
27 Lydden Road, London SW18 4LT, England
PROJECT: Lloyds of London Museum 70

Sarah Charles
78 Queensgate, London SW7 5JT, England
PROJECT: House of Shutters 164

Jim Clark Design
38 Springfield Terrace, South Queensferry EH30, Scotland
PROJECT: Halliwells House 74

Color & Design Exhibits
1911 Lundy Avenue, San José, California 95131, USA
PROJECT: Peer Logic 146

DCS Fairs Ltd
104–8 Grafton Road, London NW5 4BD, England
PROJECT: Zanders Paper 143

John Dangerfield Associates
Mantle House, Broomhill Road, London SW18 4JQ, England
PROJECTS: Belsen 1945 20–1; The Blitz Experience 18–19; The Trench Experience 16–17

David Davies Associates
12 Goslett Yard, London WC2H 0EE, England
PROJECT: The Design Museum 50–1

Design Etc Inc.
20 West 20th Street, Fourth Floor, New York City, New York 100114213, USA
PROJECTS: Buckley O'Hare 138; Don't Panic 139; Home, Future Home 46–7

Din Associates
6 South Lambeth Place, London SW8 1SP, England
PROJECTS: Pepe Jeans 160–1; Warerite 1989 152–5; Warerite 1990 156–7; Warerite BDC 158–9

Elevations
The Old School, Main Street, Denton, Northampton NN7 10Q, England
PROJECT: BBC Showcase 147

Farmer Studios Limited
16–20 Gladstone Street, Leicester, Leicestershire LE1 2BN, England
PROJECT: Roger Bacon 75

The Finsbury Partnership
44 Queensgate Terrace, London SW7 5PJ, England
PROJECT: The Crafts Council 90–1

Firbank Kempster
Holland House, 6 Church Street, Old Isleworth, London TW7 6BG, England
PROJECT: Phillips 194–5; Wang 144–5

Foley Cooke
20 Northfields Prospect, Putney Bridge Road, London SW18 1PE
PROJECTS: AGB Publications 167; Forrec 165; Interior Design Magazine 166

Josh Freeman Associates
Marketing Design Group, 8019½ Melrose Avenue, Suite 1, Los Angeles, California 90046, USA
PROJECT: Westfield Inc. 98–9

Pierre Frey
47 rue des Petits Champs, Paris 75001, France
PROJECT: Pierre Frey 179

Furneaux Stewart Design Ltd
24 Beaumont Mews, London W11N 3LN, England
PROJECTS: Citroen 205–7; Driving Ambition 214–5; Hewlett-Packard 20; Portchester Castle 90–1; Royal Northumberland Fusiliers 82–3

GLS Design
Westbrook House, 76 High Street, Alton, Hampshire GU34 1EN, England
PROJECT: Oracle 142

James Gardner (3D Concepts) Ltd
James Gardner Studio, 144 Haverstock Hill, London NW3 2AY, England
PROJECTS: National Museum of Natural Science 23; Tower of David Citadel Museum 22

Giant
A1 Riverside, Metropolitan Wharf, Wapping Wall, London E1 9SS, England
PROJECT: Read All About It 86–7

HRA
1 Union Court, Canalside, Chester CH1 3LJ, Cheshire,
England
PROJECTS: School Days 78; Street Life 79

John Hart Design Consultants
The Tannery, Gosden Common, Bramley, Guildford,
Surrey, England
PROJECT: Lloyds of London Museum 70

Carmelo Hernando Asociados SL
Perill 26, 08012 Barcelona, Spain
PROJECT: Mapasa 124–5

Dave Hobday Design
180 Kennington Park Road, London SE11 4BT,
England
PROJECTS: Citizen 100–1; Epson 198–9; Lotus 202–3;
Seikosha 197; 3M 200–1

Hornall Anderson Design Works
1008 Western, 6th Floor, Seattle, Washington 98104,
USA
PROJECT: Weyerhaeuser 196

Wayne Hunt Design Inc
87 North Raymond Avenue, Suite 215, Pasadena,
California 91103–3996, USA
PROJECT: Simpson Paper Company 104–5

Imagination
25 Store Street, South Crescent, London WC1E 7BL,
England
PROJECTS: British Telecom 126–7; Orion 212–3

Alan Irvine, Architect
2 Aubrey Place, London NW8 9BH, England
PROJECTS: The Age of Charles I 40; The Glass of the
Caesars 36–7; The Great Japan Exhibition 39–8; The
Lion of Venice 32–3; Treasures of Ancient Nigeria
30–1; Winchester Cathedral Treasury 71

Kobayashi Kogei-sha Co Ltd
1–9–15 Kita Otsuka, Toshima-ku, Tokyo, Japan
PROJECTS: Lillicolor 184–5; Kenwood 188–9

Peter Leonard Associates
535 King's Road, London SW10 OS2, England
PROJECT: Ideal Standard 178

David Mackenzie Design
Walnut House, 2 Grange Lane, Ingham, Lincolnshire
LN1 2YD, England
PROJECT: KaO Systems 117

Ingo Maurer GmbH
Kaiserstrasse 47, 8000 Munich 40, Germany
PROJECT: La Fabbrica del Vappore 174–5

Minale Tattersfield
The Courtyard, 37 Sheen Road, Richmond, Surrey
TW9 1AJ, England
PROJECT: Design Brittanico 130–1

Louis Nelson Associates Inc
80 University Place, New York City, New York 10003,
USA
PROJECT: California Wine: The Science of an Art 45

Nomura Co Ltd
4–6–4 Shibaura, Minato-ku, Tokyo 108, Japan
PROJECTS: Ohbayashi Corporation 186–7; Matsushita
Electrical Industrial Co Ltd 190–1; NEC Corporation
193; Sharp Corporation 192

The Partners
Albion Courtyard, Greenhill Rents, London EC1M
6BN, England
PROJECT: Pop! British Music in the 1980s 108–9

Pocknell and Green
Readings Farm, Blackmore End, Wethersfield, Essex
CM7 4DH, England
PROJECT: McNaughton Papers 106–7

Maurice Progin ASG
Ch. de Chandieu 22, CH 1006 Lausanne, Switzerland
PROJECT: Golay Buchel et Cie 148–9

Quod
Carles Mercader 9, 08960 Sant Just Desvern,
Barcelona, Spain
PROJECT: Aferfrans SA 150–1

John Ronayne
17 Manor Avenue, London SE4 1PE, England
PROJECTS: The Queen's House 41; Tullie House
Museum 72

Sawaya & Moroni
Piazza Missori 2, 20122 Milan, Italy
PROJECT: Sawaya & Moroni 176–7

Sayles Graphic Design
308 Eighth Street, Des Moines, Iowa 50309, USA
PROJECTS: Down on Greek Street 60–1; Iowa Power
House 58–9

Studio Works
838 Broadway, New York City, New York 10003, USA
PROJECTS: The Anatomy of a Bridge 64–5; Palace of
Commerce 66–7; Preserving Sacred Sites 119

John Sunderland Design
Troutbeck, Main Street, Allerston, Pickering, North
Yorkshire, England
PROJECT: The Jorvik Centre 73

Colin Thompson Design Associates Ltd
21–2 Warwick Street, London W1R 5RB, England
PROJECTS: Dow Chemicals Europe 123; Union Carbide
122

Trickett & Webb
The Factory, 84 Marchmont Street, London WC1N
1HE, England
PROJECTS: HarperCollins 128–9; London Brick 162–3

Williams & Phoa
2 Pear Tree Court, London EC1R 0DS, England
PROJECTS: London Docklands 118; Canary Wharf 92–
3; Paternoster 68–9

Zintzmeyer & Lux NA Inc
170 Fifth Avenue PH, New York City, New York 10010,
USA
and
Holzestrasse 33, CH 8006 Zurich, Switzerland
PROJECTS: Amsterdam Auto RAI '89 218–9;
International Motor Show 1988 214–5; North
American International Auto Show 1991 220–1;
Salon Internationale de l'Automobile 1989 216–7

Photographic Acknowledgements

p 12 **Pierre-Yves Dhinaut**; bottom left: **Jean-Pierre Gaume**; p 13 **Pierre-Yves Dhinaut**; p 14–15 **N. Faure**; p 16–21 **John Dangerfield Associates**; p 22 **James Gardner (3D Concepts) Ltd**; p 23 **Nicolas Sinclair**; p 24–7 **Peter Cook**; p 28–9 **The Trustees of the British Museum**; p 30–38 **Alan Irvine, Architect**; p 39 **The Trustees of the British Museum**; p 42–3 **The Geffrye Museum Trust**; p 44 **The National Museum of Film, Photography and Television**; p 45 **Louis Nelson Associates**; p 46–7 **Sonet**; p 48–9 **Phototèque EPPY/F.X. Bouchart**; p 50–1 **Peter Cook**; p 52–3 **Derek Adams/Natural History Photo Unit**; p 54 **Colin Keates/Natural History Photo Unit**; p 55 **Derek Adams/Natural History Photo Unit**; p 58–61 **John Sayles Graphics**; p 113–5 **The Association of Ideas**; p 116 **Peter Cook**; p 117 **Dick Mackin**; p 118 **Williams & Phoa**; p 119 **Eliot Kaufman**; p 122–3 **Acorn Studios for Colin Thompson Design**; p 124–5 **Hernandos Asociados SA**; p 126–7 **Imagination**; p 128–9 **Trickett & Webb**; p 130–1 **Minale Tattersfield**; p 132–3 **CR Communications and Design Services SA**; p 134–5 **Bowes Darby**; p 136–7 **The Association of Ideas**; p 138–9 **Bo Parker**; p 140–1 **ADSA**; p 142 **GLS Design**; p 143 **DCS Fairs Ltd**; p 144 **Publifoto/Firbank Kempster**; p 146 **Color & Design**; p 147 **Elevations**; p 148–9 **Edouard Baumgartner**; p 150–1 **Quod**; p 152–161 **Din Associates**; p 162–3 **Ian McKinnell**; p 164–5 **Sarah Charles**; p 166–7 **Foley Cooke**; p 168–173 **Achille Castiglioni**; p 174–5 **Ingo Maurer GmbH**; p 176–7 **Sawaya and Moroni**; p 178 **Peter Leonard Associates**; p 179 **Pierre Frey**; p 180 **PICTO**; p 181 **Padco Blenheim/Salons d'Interieur**; p 182 **RP Corinne Crivelli/Moving International**; p 183 **Daum/Scènes d'Interieur**; p 184–5 **Kobayashi Kogei-sha Co Ltd**; p 186–7 **Nomura Co Ltd**; p 188–9 **Kobayashi Kogei-sha Co Ltd**; p 190–1 **Nomura Co Ltd**; p 192–3 **Nomura Co Ltd**; p 194–5 **Firbank Kempster**; p 196 **Hornall Anderson Design Works**; p 197–203 **Dave Hobday Design**; p 204–211 **Furneaux Stewart**; p 212 **Imagination**; p 214–221 **Zintzmeyer & Lux AG**